JUNG'S MAP OF THE SOUL

Deeper Explorations

Murray Stein

CHIRON PUBLICATIONS • ASHEVILLE, NORTH CAROLINA

www.ChironPublications.com

Front cover painting by Diane Stanley
Interior and cover design by Danijela Mijailovic
Printed primarily in the United States of America.

ISBN 978-1-68503-690-4 paperback
ISBN 978-1-68503-691-1 hardcover
ISBN 978-1-68503-692-8 electronic
ISBN 978-1-68503-693-5 limited edition paperback
ISBN 978-1-68503-694-2 limited edition hardcover

Library of Congress Cataloging-in-Publication Data Pending

TABLE OF CONTENTS

Preface / 1

Chapter One
Ego-Consciousness and Psychological Type / 7

Chapter Two
The Unconscious: Personal and Collective / 37

Chapter Three
Persona, Shadow, Anima and Animus / 67

Chapter Four
Psychic Energy / 93

Chapter Five
The Individuation Process / 113

Chapter Six
The Self / 137

Chapter Seven
Synchronicity and Meaning / 155

Chapter Eight
Jungian Psychoanalysis – A Brief Account / 169

References / 187

Preface

To begin, I want to thank Len Cruz and Steve Buser of Chiron Publications for their suggestion that I write this updated version of my earlier book, *Jung's Map of the Soul*. Their words of encouragement were inspirational and offered a welcome opportunity to take my reflections on Jung's "map" some steps further to what I hope the reader will find to be a deeper level of exploration, hence the title of this book. It has now been over a quarter of a century since the earlier version was published, and much expansion and further development has taken place in the field of Jungian psychology since then.

In addition, the adaptation of some ideas from that book by the wildly popular K-Pop group, BTS, for several of their best-selling albums has given me added motivation to update this work and offer further reflections to a new generation of readers. It has been my hope for decades that Jung's insights into the human mind would be as widely disseminated as possible in the global community of soul-searchers and thinkers.

In the earlier book, which was based on lectures I delivered at the Jung Center in Evanston, Illinois in 1991, I offered an introduction to the fundamental theories of analytical psychology as presented in several central texts in the *Collected Works of C.G. Jung*. Those sources remain important for what is presented here, but today it is possible to include many further texts by Jung that were not available at that time. Previously unpublished letters and the seminars given by Jung in the 1920s and 1930s have appeared that add fascinating complexity, allowing further understanding of his thinking. The correspondences with Victor White, Wolfgang Pauli, and Erich Neumann offer fascinating insights into Jung's developing thoughts about religion, physics, and analytical psychology. And the brilliant seminars—*Dream Analysis*, *Visions*, *Nietzsche's Zarathustra,* and *Children's Dreams*—feature Jung speaking vividly and freely (and often humorously) to small audiences of enthralled colleagues and students at the Psychology Club in Zurich. These carefully edited books offer a wealth of information for a renewed and even revised appreciation of Jung's incredible range of interests and his remarkable capacity for playful and imaginative thinking.

Most important to mention are the publications of *The Red Book: Liber Novus* in 2009 and the *Black*

Books in 2020. These books made the private writings of Jung available to the public, and they have added considerably to our understanding of the creation of his map of the soul. The characters, landscapes, and ideas that Jung discovered in his own deep dive into the dark waters of the unconscious, and his recording of his experiences initially in the *Black Books* before writing out and amplifying the text for *Liber Novus* and finally transcribing it in *The Red Book*, offer us a view into much of the background of his later theoretical writings. In his meticulously crafted calligraphic script and his colorful paintings and illustrations, Jung created a timeless work of art, capturing his exploration of his inner world during his midlife period—an era in his life that the historian Henri Ellenberger called a "creative illness." Jung's hand-scripted *Red Book* was left unfinished when he abandoned further work on it in 1928, but the inner explorations that the publication of *The Red Book: Liber Novus* made visible to readers today are invaluable for our study of the map he later created in his official writings and seminars. In recognition of its importance, my late friend Thomas Arzt and I invited seventy Jungian scholars and analysts to contribute essays, which we published in five volumes under the series title *Jung's Red Book for Our Time: Searching for Soul Under Post-Modern Conditions* (Chiron Publications, 2017–2022).

Additionally, since the first edition of *Jung's Map of the Soul* was published in 1998, a large number of publications by many Jungian authors have extended and deepened our understanding of Jung's oeuvre. In this book, I am offering further reflections that include the views of many other gifted scholars. For their contributions, I express my deepest appreciation and gratitude.

Most of Jung's texts are so multilayered and complex that one can read them many times with an ever deeper and more capacious understanding of his vision and how he was using his multitude of sources—ancient, medieval, and modern. In my own recent readings, I have attended more carefully than before to footnotes, particularly in the alchemical writings, which show a highly complex and intimate web of relations between Jungian psychology and the philosophical and religious ideas of often obscure and esoteric texts from medieval and ancient times. Jung was very concerned with connecting modern depth psychology to the wisdom of the cultural traditions out of which it grew. Modern psychology is a product of the European Enlightenment and of scientific thinkers, many of whom had no interest whatsoever in the cultural roots of their discipline. For Jung, it was essential to become conscious of this history. This was the rationale for his extensive study and writing on Gnostic and alchemical sources. It was more than a serious hobby for Jung; it was fundamental to his oeuvre.

This new account of Jung's map of the soul represents my own further study concerning the many layers and levels embedded in Jung's thinking about the human psyche. I only hope and pray I can do justice to the rich legacy he has left us.

I want to thank Jennifer Fitzgerald for her assistance in bringing this book to print. I also want to thank my family, patients, colleagues, and friends, with whom I have shared many of these thoughts over the years, and especially Diane Stanley for her brilliant cover design for this book.

Chapter One

Ego-Consciousness and Psychological Type

While on board an ocean liner returning home from the United States in 1909 with Sigmund Freud, Jung had a dream that would guide his future thinking about the psyche. He dreamed that he was on the upper floor of an unfamiliar two-story house, although it was declared to be "my house," as he wrote in *Memories, Dreams, Reflections.*[1] He looked around and saw that the room was decorated nicely in the rococo style with old masters hanging on the walls. Very nice, he thought to himself. But he did not know what was on the floor below, and being the explorer he was, he decided to have a look. The ground floor, he discovered, was rather dark, older than the upper floor, and decorated in a medieval style.

[1] C.G. Jung, *Memories, Dreams, Reflections*, p. 158.

This really aroused his curiosity, and he set out to discover more about this interesting house that he found himself occupying. Opening a heavy door, he saw a stone stairway going down to the cellar. He descended into a beautiful ancient room with a vaulted ceiling and realized that it was ancient, dating from Roman times. Now intensely curious, he studied the stone slabs on the floor and spotted a ring fixed into one of them. This opened to a stairway of narrow stone steps, and when he walked carefully down them, he entered a low cave carved into the rock at the foundations of the house. Dust lay on the floor and bones were scattered about, along with two skulls and broken pieces of pottery. This was obviously a prehistoric space. He had reached the bottom of this house's history. This dream, Jung wrote in *Memories, Dreams, Reflections*, "was important to me, for it led me for the first time to the concept of the 'collective unconscious' and thus formed a kind of prelude to my book, *Wandlungen und Symbole der Libido*."[2] It was this book that broke Jung's by-now fragile relationship with Freud and freed him to create an image of the psyche that would be uniquely his

[2] Ibid.

own. Jung, no longer a Freudian, could now become a Jungian.

In this discussion of the map of the soul that Jung pieced together, step by step, I will explore these levels in the house that Jung discovered in his dream of 1909. To begin, I will describe what Jung wrote about the upper level of the two-story house, representing the space of ego-consciousness.

Ego-Consciousness

The terms "ego" and "consciousness" belong together and are inseparable in Jung's understanding, as we shall see. Psychic contents are held in consciousness by virtue of their relation to the ego. Also, as Jung pithily declared, "there is no will [i.e., ego] without consciousness."[3] Ego and consciousness are dependent on one another. This is why Jung generally referred to "ego-consciousness" in his writings. One can separate the terms linguistically for analytic purposes, but in reality they are two parts or aspects of a single "complex."

The Latin pronoun *ego* is a term of common usage in the English language. It is generally associated with

[3] C.G. Jung, *The Solar Myths and Opicinus de Canistris*, p. 86.

selfishness, as in expressions like, "He has a big ego." The word denotes a negative evaluation and is contrasted with positive values such as altruism and compassion, which imply care for others and not primarily for oneself. Saints are "without ego," as people speak of them. Schools of spirituality work to "get rid of ego" and replace it with an attitude that is more compassionate and less self-centered. In Jungian psychology, however, "ego" is a neutral term and means only "I," as in the original Latin.

English use of the Latin word *ego* began in the eighteenth century, with psychologists and philosophers using "the ego" instead of "the I" to refer to this aspect of subjectivity. German language writers, on the other hand, did not use the Latin term in their corresponding works. When these philosophers and psychologists, including Freud and Jung, wrote about the subject, they used the common German first-person pronoun, *das Ich*. However, when their works were translated into English, *Ich* was translated as "ego" and not as "I." This was consistent with the practice in English medical texts, which used Latin words and phrases as technical terms, whereas German-speaking scientific writers used vernacular German words for the purpose.

In psychoanalytic writings, both German and English languages turn a pronoun into a noun: *Ich* becomes *das Ich*, and "ego" becomes "the ego." This objectifies the subject and makes it into a suitable object for scientific inquiry. Normally, people use the word "I" to speak of their conscious subjective feelings, wishes, desires, thoughts, intentions, and so forth. When psychologists analyze them, they observe the person's subjectivity from an objective outsider's position and call it "the ego." In short, "the ego" is the subject seen as an object.

In Jung's analysis of the psyche, the ego occupies the position of center in the wide field of consciousness. This complex dwells on the upper-story of the house of the psyche and typically claims authority over the whole house, without knowing much, if anything, about all the other occupants on lower floors. The ego lives more or less comfortably in this space, in the company of the other family members on the same level. It is the central actor with the responsibility to maintain order at this level of the house, and to represent the family in the community.

The ego is not only an actor, however, but also the primary self-reflexive agent of the personality. Subjective self-awareness is its gift. This is a unique quality and indeed a miraculous feature of the personality that sets the human psyche apart from technical or artificial intelligence. A child is born with a germ of this ego potential, which grows according to its innately given capacities, alongside physical and psychological development. At a certain moment, the "I" takes note of its own existence, and the ego's gift of self-awareness to the field of consciousness is born. It is as if a light is turned on in consciousness. Jung recounted such an experience when he was around the age of twelve:

> I was taking the long road to school from Klein Hüningen, where we lived, to Basel, when suddenly for a single moment, I had the overwhelming impression of having just emerged from a dense cloud. I knew all at once: now I am *myself*! It was as if a wall of mist were at my back, and behind that wall, there was not yet an "I." But at this moment, I came upon *myself.* Previously I had existed, too, but everything had merely happened to me. Now I happened to myself. Now I knew: I am myself now, now I exist. Previously I had been willed to do this and that, now *I* willed. This experience seemed to me tremendously important and new: there was "authority" in me.[4]

[4] C.G. Jung, *Memories, Dreams, Reflections*, pp. 32–33.

The ego in Jung's personality suddenly became self-aware. The realization that he existed now as an individual, a center of will and authority, was experienced as coming out of a cloud of unknowing. In this moment, Jung discovered himself to be not only an actor playing an assigned role, but also an actor who knew himself to be an actor and what kind of role he was playing. It gave him a sense of power and authority over the course his life would take. This is self-consciousness. Now, he could even choose to change his role. In a moment like this, a sense of self-identity is awakened.

The word "will" is important in understanding the ego as a conscious agent. One's subjective experience is that the "I" has "free will"—that is, the ability to make choices by conscious intention and not only by conditioning and learned habits. The philosophy of Existentialism is based on the presupposition that one can create a personal destiny by making choices freely. This is a view of ego capacity as liberated from cultural, theological (God's will), or other constraining forces, such as those of astrology (the planets). The perspective holds that fate (*heimarmene* in the Greek) is a fiction and the individual ego has the capacity to forge its own destiny. For more than a century, this philosophy has held strong appeal, as people have increasingly abandoned religious faith in higher powers. Friedrich Nietzsche, in the persona of the prophet Zarathustra, announced the death of God and celebrated the liberated *Übermensch* ("higher man"). This was an extension of European humanism, which proclaimed that the individual could make their own meaning. Jung's experience on the road to Basel was an adolescent version of this birth of the modern ego. From then on, he was not contained in the Christian myth of his forefathers.

Later in life, when he became a psychologist, Jung would contend that analytical psychology could demonstrate that this view of the ego's freedom exaggerates the extent of free will and liberation from other factors in the house of the psyche. In fact, there are many subtle constraints and influences that determine choice to a much larger extent than is generally acknowledged by the ego. Nietzsche's "higher man" represents the pathology of "inflation," or what Jung called the "mana personality."[5] This is a dangerous illusion on the part of the ego. Many ego decisions and choices are heavily influenced by the unconscious conditioning of family, education, and culture. Moreover, the psychological complexes that live on the lower levels of the house, as I will discuss

[5] C.G. Jung, *Two Essays on Analytical Psychology*, paras. 374ff.

in later chapters, play a critical role in influencing one's preferences, thereby undermining one's supposed freedom to choose rationally and freely from among the alternatives presented. While people may feel and think that they are making free choices, they are in fact mostly following age-old tracks and grooves in the psyche that have been laid down in childhood and beyond—over centuries and millennia.

The feeling of having a free-willing and authoritative "I" is intoxicating for the ego. "Now I have *authority*," as Jung wrote of his boyhood experience of discovering self-awareness. In the West, having such an experience of the ego and feeling an inner center of personal authority is considered a requirement for mental health. This is a bedrock of theory and practice in much of Western psychology and psychotherapy. The East, on the other hand, questions whether this "ego" exists and believes that Westerners live in a state of delusion and false consciousness. This is not to deny consciousness, only "I-centered consciousness." A Japanese person might write, "Going down the road, turn left," while a European would write, "I am going down a road, and I turn left." The ego is in charge of the action and the act of writing about it. Western practice has created a substance of something that is merely referential—a pronoun. In English, in fact, the pronoun I is always capitalized, while other pronouns (you, we, us, them, etc.) are not. "I" is a King or Queen; the rest are commoners. About East Asian cultures, one sometimes speaks about a "we-ego" rather than an "I-ego." The "we-ego" includes others in the center of consciousness. It is a group consciousness—or better said, it is consciousness of the "I" as a member of a group, and not as an individual.

In fact, the "I" is a very elusive psychic entity. If one goes about one's daily life doing the usual tasks—working at a job, driving a car, paying bills, exercising, and so forth—one is not usually aware of an "I" who is acting. One just acts without self-consciousness. The German philosopher Martin Heidegger called this *dasein* ("being there"). We don't think, "Oh, I am doing this," or, "Now I am doing that." The "I" is not in the foreground of awareness. Where is it? When we look at these same activities objectively from the outside (as psychologists), we assume that something is directing them. In the case of animals, we might say that the director is instinct; regarding humans, we tend to think it is at least partially the ego acting out of its surplus of free will. The individual is held accountable for their actions, whether it is an act of courage, such as leading the charge on a battlefield, or a heinous crime, like rape or murder. To what degree this supposition is correct must be analyzed in each case. The extent of free choice by ego-consciousness that is operative in one's activities varies a great deal from person to person and according to psychological conditions such as post-traumatic stress disorder. A particular action may be routine activity that is done without much ego or consciousness, or it may be "mindful"—that is to say, consciously intended and directed. In the latter case, the ego is awake and consciously involved, and therefore held responsible under law.

Of the ego, Jung wrote: "By ego, I understand a complex of ideas which constitutes the center of my field of consciousness and appears to possess a high degree of continuity and identity."[6] Important to note in this defining statement are the phrases "complex of ideas" and "field of consciousness." As "a complex of *ideas*," the ego rests on "a fundamental, *a priori* factor."[7] Jung used the term "idea" in the Platonic sense, describing that the ego is made up of psychic material that is timeless and unchanging (i.e., "ideas"). The "field of consciousness," on the other hand, consists of psychic material that is temporal—thoughts, feelings, memories, and observations that accumulate around the central

[6] C.G. Jung, *Psychological Types*, para. 706.
[7] Ibid., para. 756.

ego during an individual's life. Ego-consciousness thus includes features that are both eternal and temporal. The full field of ego-consciousness is the result of a process that gathers bits and pieces of experience around an archetypal core and fuses them into an "identity," a sense of "me-ness." These pieces are taken up into ego-consciousness through a process of projection and introjection, which is based on *participation mystique*, or identification with the object.[8] Consciousness consists of psychic contents that are related to the ego "in so far as this relation is perceived as such by the ego,"[9] and this connectedness of contents to the ego expands a sense of identity over time. The presence of the ego in consciousness brings the "for-me-ness" feeling that is spoken of by investigators of consciousness as its essential feature.[10]

The ego also becomes identified with the body, for some people more closely than for others. The body belongs to one's "me-ness." It is "my body." One can separate oneself from the body to some extent, but the ego remains intractably associated with the body to a

---

[8] Ibid., para. 741.
[9] Ibid., para. 700.
[10] L. Stein and M. Stein, "The Role of the Brain in Individuation," p. 462.

degree, except in instances of severe dissociation, as occurs in near death experiences. When the ego thinks or feels that the body is threatened with death, it feels similarly threatened with annihilation.

In what sense does the ego "develop" if it is made up of timeless "ideas"? Psychologists and psychotherapists often speak and write about "ego development." A young child of two or three will say, "I want, I will." Before the child can speak, it will reach for what it wants. The child's actions show agency, and the psychologist will interpret this as evidence of an early ego, in that it shows the quality of "for-me-ness." From this beginning in action, there follows a sense of self-awareness of the ego as agent. The ego eventually becomes objective about itself and can mirror itself. This is the miracle of human consciousness. From this position of objectivity, the ego can begin to become aware of the great Self of which it is but a part. This is another step in the ego's development—the process of becoming conscious of who and what one is. Jung named this process "individuation," which I will discuss in greater detail in a later chapter.

In his final book, *Mysterium Coniunctionis*, Jung wrote: "our consciousness issues from a dark body, the ego, which is the indispensable condition for all consciousness."[11] This "dark body" is "a highly complex affair full of unfathomable obscurities."[12] He defines it as "a relatively constant personification of the unconscious itself."[13] The ego's development, then, relies on its becoming conscious of its sources in the unconscious—the unconscious sources of one's being. We see an early example of this in the twelve-year-old Jung who suddenly became aware of himself as "I am." This step in ego development created separation and broke his identification with the surrounding world. Much later in life, Jung speculated that the creation of ego-consciousness for all of humanity also proceeded from a similar starting point.

"That is the world, and this is I: That was the first morning of the world, the first sunrise after the primal darkness, when that inchoately conscious complex the ego, the son of the darkness, knowingly sundered subject and object, and thus precipitated the world and itself into definite existence, giving it and itself a voice and a name."[14]

[11] C.G. Jung, *Mysterium Coniunctionis*, para. 129.
[12] Ibid.
[13] Ibid.
[14] Ibid.

The ego functions as the *principium individuationis* of the psyche, as Jung's Gnostic teacher, Basilides of Alexandria (aka Philemon in *Liber Novus*), speaks of this principle in Sermon I of *Septem Sermones ad Mortuos* ("Seven Sermons to the Dead").[15] The ego makes distinctions in consciousness ("the effective and the ineffective, fullness and emptiness, living and dead, light and darkness"[16]), and draws a line of separation between itself and the other. This type of activity on the part of the ego continues throughout life, because the contents of the unconscious continue to be projected into objects, and this requires the ego to go on making distinctions. As a consequence of this ego activity, the individual becomes ever aware of being a discrete, unique personality. "At-one-ness" with the surroundings, inner and outer, is sacrificed to "for-me-ness." At the extreme, this becomes ego-centrism.

On the other hand, the ego holds the objects surrounding it in consciousness, and this holding-together makes ongoing relationships possible: "By consciousness I understand the relation of psychic

---

[15] C.G. Jung, *Memories, Dreams, Reflections*, p. 380; *The Red Book: Liber Novus*: *A Reader's Edition*, p. 512.

[16] C.G. Jung, *Memories, Dreams, Reflections*, p. 380.

contents to the ego."[17] Consciousness depends on the presence of an ego, which forms a magnetic center. For a content of the psyche to become part of consciousness, the ego must first perceive it: "Relations to the ego that are not perceived as such are unconscious."[18] The ego maintains consciousness by holding people, places, and things together in a perceived network of object relations, making distinctions among them and organizing them according to the rules of typology (more on the role of psychological types in ego functioning in a moment). Conversely, consciousness is responsible for maintaining the relation to the ego: "Consciousness is the function or activity which maintains the relation of psychic contents to the ego."[19] Maintenance of ego-consciousness is thus a two-way operation: the ego perceives psychic contents, and consciousness maintains the connection to the ego. This cooperative effort creates relative stability in ego-consciousness.

When contents in ego-consciousness become unattached from the ego for some reason, they drop off into the darkness of the unconscious. Freud attributed this loss of contact to repression. Some contents of consciousness,

[17] C.G. Jung, *Psychological Types*, para. 700.
[18] Ibid.
[19] Ibid.

like memories of traumatic experiences, create painful emotions and are therefore deleted. They disappear into the unconscious, where they remain active but only show themselves in dreams or sudden flashbacks. Jung did not disagree with this view, but he added that some contents of ego-consciousness just fall away of their own weight (i.e., are forgotten). The ego can pull some of these back into consciousness through an effort to remember or associate, though some simply disappear and are never thought of again. They vanish into the vast psychic area unknown to the conscious mind—the unconscious.

An ego can be strong and resilient, or weak and fragile. A strong ego is generally taken to be one that can bear conflict and suffering without turning away from the light of perception and becoming defensive by resorting to repression or dissociation. It can endure painful feelings, hold them, contain them, and work with them in psychotherapy. Psychotherapy seeks to strengthen the ego so it can bear the suffering that is inevitably part of life. If the ego cannot bear the suffering and utilizes defenses to delete it from consciousness, its cause does not go away, but lingers at the fringes of consciousness and emerges in dreams, waking fantasies, anxieties, or depressions. If accepted, one can give these contents a decent burial and move on in life, all the while remembering and respecting them—from a distance.

A weak ego is one that resorts excessively to defense mechanisms. Ego defenses are a natural part of the ego's equipment for survival, because it has only a limited capacity to absorb reality. The ego is called a "reality function" because it gathers information about what it perceives to be going on in the world around and within. A weak ego turns away and does not want to know very much, because it cannot bear or contain it. Thus, ego defenses quickly come into play and block those perceptions, thoughts, and feelings from consciousness, like how the ostrich that puts its head in the sand when it sees trouble ahead. The weak ego is fragile, susceptible to dissociating and breaking into pieces. In one of his reflections on the ego in *The Psychology of the Transference*, Jung wrote:

> A certain *abaissement du niveau mental*, i.e., a weakness in the hierarchical order of the ego, is enough to set… instinctive urges and desires in motion and bring about a dissociation of personality – in other words, a multiplication of its centers of gravity.[20]

[20] C.G. Jung, "The Psychology of the Transference," para. 361.

When the ego is fragile—and it can be rendered such by illness, drugs, or fatigue—it can be brought to a breaking point and fragment. At that point, when the ego can no longer direct the will, instinctive urges and desires become dominant. Ever present in the unconscious, they are given an opening to flood into consciousness and take control of emotions and behavior. Instincts such as hunger, sexuality, activity, manic creativity, and obsessive-compulsive reflection will take over the personality, leaving the individual helpless and unable to resist their pressures.

A strong ego can manage such instinctive pressures more or less successfully—satisfying them enough while still curbing their pressure and keeping them in check. However, when the ego is weak and instinctual pressures mount, a dissociation takes place and, as Jung wrote, a multiplication of "centers of gravity" ensues. There is now not one ego but several, which are fragments of the formerly intact ego. This creates a state of confusion in consciousness, as its focal center shifts from one ego state, to another, to another. A person in this condition becomes confused about who they are, where they are, what they want or do not want, and so forth. The normal ego capacities of controlling and governing the mind and behavior fade, and the instincts take over.

The Miracle of Consciousness

On the topic of consciousness, Jung described it as a kind of miracle. In the entry for "Consciousness" in the Glossary of *Memories, Dreams, Reflections*, Aniela Jaffé quoted from the "Basel Seminar" of 1934 as follows:

> When one reflects upon what consciousness really is, one is profoundly impressed by the extreme wonder of the fact that an event which takes place outside in the cosmos simultaneously produces an internal image. It takes place, so to speak, inside as well, which is to say becomes conscious.[21]

In a similar vein, Jung wrote in his extemporaneous 1943 Eranos seminar, "The Solar Myths and Opicinus de Canistris":

> Precisely, consciousness has a meaning that is entirely extraordinary. It is really the world. Without consciousness, nothing exists. The world had really been nothing at all until somebody said: that is the world; that is. As

[21] C.G. Jung, *Memories, Dreams, Reflections*, p. 394.

> long as that was not known, the world was really entirely superfluous.[22]

Jung appreciated both the mystery and the gift of consciousness. The extraordinary thing is that the outer world and the world of consciousness coincide. When the light goes on outside, something goes on inside and one starts seeing things. Those things that one sees are both external and internal, but primarily they belong to consciousness. One does not really see the world as it is. One sees images of the world that are recorded by the senses and sent to the brain, and the brain makes pictures of the sensory data and offers them to consciousness. So, when the light goes on, the outer world becomes bright and consciousness takes note of the world as imaged by the brain.

The miracle of consciousness is something that Jung the psychologist often marveled at. *Memories, Dreams, Reflections* describes an experience of enlightenment he had in 1925, at the age of fifty. He had given himself the birthday present of a trip with friends to Africa for a couple of months. Standing on a hill and looking out at

[22] C.G. Jung, *The Solar Myths and Opicinus de Canistris*, p. 86.

a vast plane with animals walking around, eating, taking their natural ease, he realized:

> There I was now, the first human being to recognize that this was the world, but who did not know that in this moment he had first really created it. There the cosmic meaning of consciousness became overwhelmingly clear to me. "What nature leaves imperfect, the art perfects," say the alchemists. Man, I, in an invisible act of creation put the stamp of perfection on the world by giving it objective existence.[23]

That is the meaning of human life in the universe. Humans have been endowed with consciousness to make the cosmos conscious of itself.

Jung incorporated this insight into much of his later work, and especially his quasi-theological thinking, as found in *Answer to Job*. Schopenhauer spoke of consciousness as a mirror to the world. Indeed, human consciousness mirrors back to the unconscious forces, which created the cosmos, what they have done. In

[23] C.G. Jung, *Memories, Dreams, Reflections*, pp. 255–256.

theological language, Jung wrote that God needs humans to become conscious, and humans add consciousness to God's creativity. God is creative, humans are conscious, and humans can make God conscious of what has been created, showing it to the Divine. In this way, Jung surmised, humans add value to the cosmos. That is our gift and our role in the universe: consciousness.

While Jung often spoke that consciousness is limited and much smaller than the unconscious, which is vast and without boundaries, he did not discount its value, nor did he undervalue the role of the ego in psychic life. The ego mirrors the unconscious and therefore can make it conscious, to a degree. Consciousness makes the world, inner and outer, conscious of itself.

The ego orients itself—to the world around, to social relationships, to family members, to friends, to a workplace—by adopting what Jung called a "persona." This will be discussed in detail in chapter five. The persona is a feature of ego-functioning that adapts to the expectations of the surrounding world. Some people find it quite difficult to establish a persona in interpersonal and group situations, so their ego is unable to play an appropriate role. There is a lack of socialization. In such cases, clinicians may speak of the person as being "on the spectrum," in reference to Autism Spectrum Disorder (ASD). ASD is characterized by a deficiency in adaptation to the social environment that leaves the ego stranded in isolation and unable to make correct judgments about social behavior that fits the situation. This often leads to aggressive behavior or withdrawal. Introversion is sometimes mistakenly diagnosed as ASD, but it is not considered pathological.

Psychological Type

One of Jung's largest books among the eighteen volumes of the *Collected Works* is volume six, entitled *Psychological Types*. There, Jung lays out a theory of ego "functions" and "attitudes" that govern perception and mental reality-construction. There are four psychological functions (sensation, intuition, thinking, and feeling) and two psychological attitudes (extroversion and introversion). These are tools that the ego uses to navigate its way through the world, to make sense of inner and outer objects and subjects, and to interpret and adjust to what it finds.

Jung developed his theory of psychological types in response to the widely differing theories of Sigmund Freud and Alfred Adler concerning neurosis. Freud, he found, focused on desire for the external object. The sexual instinct was thought to respond to a perceived object of attraction and want to use the object for pleasure. Viewed through this lens of the pleasure principle, Freud's psyche could be said to be basically extroverted and oriented toward the outer object of desire. Adler's theory, on the other hand, viewed the psyche through a lens concerned with subjective feelings of superiority and inferiority and the need for power. A person's innate inferiority feelings as a small being in an overwhelmingly large and threatening world were thought to be compensated by a superiority attitude. This theory was based on an interior world of subjectivity and a consequent attempt by the ego to dominate the external world. Jung saw this as a psychology based on introversion.

Reflecting on this contrast between the two types of thinking (as exemplified by Freud and Adler), Jung concluded that the attitude (extraversion or introversion) of the author shaped their theories. He wrote in 1929: "Our psychology is the more or less successfully formulated confession of a few individuals."[24] Extroverts see human nature and the psyche in one way, while introverts see it another way. The ego prefers one over the other.

To these two psychological attitudes Jung added four psychological functions to complete his typology.

[24] C.G. Jung, "Freud and Jung: Contrasts," para. 772.

This full theory of "types" was developed over several years, in vigorous discussion with colleagues such as Hans Schmid,[25] until it was finally published in 1921 as *Psychological Types*. The four functions are divided into two non-irrational (sensation and intuition) and two rational (thinking and feeling). Sensation and intuition perceive the external world in the extroverted attitude, and the inner world of images and impulses in the introverted attitude. In doing so, sensation uses the five senses while intuition receives information from the unconscious. Intuition is very fast-moving in perceiving what is going to happen next and what is possible, looking ahead, whereas sensation moves more slowly and deliberately, looking to the present—to what exists now.

The two rational functions, thinking and feeling, are opposites to each other, as are sensation and intuition. Thinking uses the mind's cognitive abilities. It is logos-based and organizes conscious material in a logical way, structuring it according to rules and principles (cognitive frameworks) to draw maps and conclusions. Feeling, on its part, refers not to emotions, but to values. Jung called

[25] For details, see D. Bair, *Jung. A Biography*, pp. 278ff.; J. Beebe and E. Falzeder (eds.), *The Question of Psychological Types*.

it a "valuing function." It is rational, in that it formulates values according to fundamental principles grounded in psyche. However, while thinking is neutral about value, feeling introduces basic values into ego-consciousness. At its highest level, it is an ethical function.

The combination of function and attitude in a person yields one of eight "psychological types": extraverted or introverted thinking, feeling, intuition, or sensation. In the Myers-Briggs Type Inventory (MBTI) system, the same functions and attitudes are clustered in further combinations, yielding superior, auxiliary, tertiary, and inferior pairs. Jungian psychoanalyst John Beebe has done a great deal of further work in explaining conscious and unconscious combinations. The main idea is that the ego has at its disposal a preferred and a less preferred attitude and function, and it uses its preferred combination to orient itself and proceed through the world in a characteristic way. The ego may prefer, for example, extroverted feeling and introverted intuition. With extroverted feeling, it will make value judgments; with introverted intuition, it will delve into spiritual perspectives. Ego-consciousness will be guided by these combinations in making choices about important decisions—about one's vocation, partnerships, hobbies, and so forth. The ego's free will is oriented and constrained by these tools at its disposal.

Typological preferences run deep and play an important part in forming an individual's character. What determines them is unknown and sometimes accredited to genetic inheritance or to a combination of genetics and social conditioning, with the former being considered the more dominant factor. In any individual, the attitude and functions that are unconscious or less developed (what we call the "inferior functions") belong to the shadow, therefore inhabiting a lower story of the psyche's house. At times, they can break through into ego-consciousness and take over the personality in an *enantiodromic* (reversal of type) movement, resulting in a state of "possession." Suddenly a business executive will become a manic picture painter. They have never paid much attention to art previously, but all of a sudden everything is about color and form, and they have to buy a large assortment of paint materials and start painting, because that's where life and energy is. It has been neglected, but now it has become activated and taken over the ego. The so-called free will of the ego is harnessed to the compulsion that comes from the unconscious.

The creation and maintenance of ego-consciousness as a stable feature of the personality is a very complex process. A lot of the work that Jungian psychoanalysts do with clients has to do with ego-strengthening.

Patients bring problems, and the therapist reflects with them about their emotional troubles and tries to reorient their ego so they can function more successfully in their conscious lives. Jungian psychoanalysts do not neglect this aspect of treatment, but their ultimate goal is to explore the deeper levels of the many-storied house of the psyche and to bring consciousness to the whole.

Chapter Two

The Unconscious: Personal and Collective

While it is certainly true that Jung regarded ego-consciousness with great respect as a central feature of human psychology, his main interest from the time he was a medical student at the University of Basel was the unconscious. In 1897, he gave a lecture to his fellow fraternity brothers in the Zofingia Society entitled "Some Thoughts on Psychology," in which he argued passionately for a type of psychology that would include the idea of an unconscious psyche that governs instinctual patterns of behavior.[26] It is evident that Jung had been studying German psychology and philosophy in some depth, despite being enrolled officially in the Medical School. In his Zofingia talk, he cited the

[26] C.G. Jung, "Some Thoughts on Psychology," para. 178.

work of the great German philosopher Immanuel Kant, whom he quoted on "an indissoluble communion with all the immaterial natures of the spirit world, alternately affecting these natures and receiving impressions from them."[27] This line spoke to Jung deeply, and in his lecture he was caustic in his criticism of rationalistic psychology and on fire in his advocacy for a view of the human mind consisting not only of ego-consciousness, but also of a hidden, invisible, subtle dimension commonly referred to as "the unconscious." When he was studying for his medical final examinations and read the Preface to Richard Krafft-Ebing's textbook *Lehrbuch der Psychiatrie,* it struck him that he would find what he was searching for in the specialty of psychiatry:

> My heart began suddenly to pound. I had to stand up and draw a deep breath. My excitement was intense, for it had become clear to me, in a flash of illumination, that for me the only possible goal as psychiatry. Here alone the two currents of my interest could flow together and in united stream dig their own bed. Here was the empirical field common to biological

[27] Ibid., para. 107.

> and spiritual facts, which I everywhere sought and nowhere found. Here at last was the place where the collision of nature and spirit became a reality.[28]

This sudden realization led Jung into the field of psychiatry and his lifelong investigation into the structure and dynamics of the unconscious—the lower levels of the house he dreamed about on his journey with Freud in 1909.

The history of the notion of the unconscious has been studied extensively by students of philosophy, psychology, and dynamic psychiatry.[29] Foremost among these has been Henri Ellenberger, whose magisterial work, *The Discovery of the Unconscious,* traces the story from the anthropological studies of indigenous peoples to the usage made of this term in dynamic psychiatry to the psychoanalytic theories of Freud, Adler, and Jung. The idea of an unconscious area of the mind took hold in European thought in the eighteenth and (especially) nineteenth centuries in Germany and France. Leading figures who Jung studied and referenced in many of

[28] C.G. Jung, *Memories, Dreams, Reflections*, pp. 108–109.
[29] For an account of this history, see S. Shamdasani, *Jung and the Making of Modern Psychology*.

his works include C.G. Carus, the German medical doctor and philosopher who wrote a book entitled *Psyche* (1846), and Eduard von Hartmann, the German philosopher who wrote *Philosophy of the Unconscious* (1869).

These thinkers influenced Jung's understanding of the unconscious even more so than Freud, whose view on the topic he encountered in 1900 through *The Interpretation of Dreams*. In an interview with Ximena de Angulo, Jung, when asked about the importance of Freud for his use of the term "unconscious," replied: "I had these thoughts long before I came to Freud. *Unconscious* is an *epistemological* term deriving from von Hartmann. Freud was not much of a philosopher, he was strictly a medical man. I had read these philosophers long before I ever saw Freud. I came to Freud for facts."[30] What impressed Jung about Freud's thought in *The Interpretation of Dreams* was: "here is a man who was not just theorizing away, here is a man who has got *facts*."[31]

Since the publication of Ellenberger's landmark book in 1970, more work has been done on the historical

[30] X. de Angelo, "Comments on a Doctoral Thesis," p. 208.
[31] Ibid.

background of Jung's use of the philosophical concept of the unconscious. Sonu Shamdasani's study *Jung and the Making of Modern Psychology* sharpens and summarizes the background, and the study by Sean McGrath on the philosophy of Friedrich Schelling and his contemporaries, entitled *The Dark Ground of Spirit: Schelling and the Unconscious*, deepens our understanding of this philosophical heritage. Jung himself frequently mentioned Arthur Schopenhauer as another strong influence on his thinking about the role of the unconscious in the psyche. It is certain that he read Schopenhauer's *The World as Will and Representation* carefully and absorbed many of Schopenhauer's ideas about the centrality of the unconscious "will" as the source of psychic energy ("libido") and in creating the mind's representations of the world. Freud offered "facts" of a more specific kind, as Jung observed, and brought the philosopher's views of the unconscious to bear on the interpretation of dreams. Jung, in his own work, would combine philosophy and facts to create his unique psychological theories.

The unconscious shows itself in a variety of ways. The classic forms are dreams and projections, visions and hallucinations. Another form that fascinated Jung was the occult, such as the practice of communicating with the dead. As a psychologist, he would refrain from granting the spirits of the dead metaphysical reality; instead, he considered their appearances psychological phenomena (i.e., manifestations of the unconscious). The "spirits" were inhabitants of the lower levels of the psychic house—which level was to be determined.

In the ancient world, necromantic conversations with the spirits of the dead were considered a means of discerning the future and making plans accordingly. Odysseus made a journey to the Underworld to speak with the blind seer Tiresias, who gave him advice on how to find his way home and what to do when he got there. Aeneas made a similar journey to the Land of the Dead and had a conversation there with his deceased beloved father, Anchises, who told him about his future. "I'll reveal the future glory of our Trojan lineage… I'll teach you your destiny,"[32] Anchises said to his son.

This type of conversation with ancestral spirits was familiar to Jung in his own family. His grandfather, Samuel Preiswerk, the distinguished Antistes at the Cathedral in Basel, conversed regularly with his deceased wife, and Jung's cousin, Helene ("Helly") Preiswerk, was a gifted medium who could contact the family's ancestral spirits and speak in the tone and

[32] Virgil, *The Aeneid*, Bk. 6, lines 756–759.

accent of their voices. Séances, set up by his mother on certain days of the week, were regularly held in Jung's childhood home, and Helly would come to them and perform. The curtains would be drawn, the room darkened, and family members would sit with her around a table as it would begin to shake and levitate. Helly would go into a trance and begin speaking in the voices of dead ancestors, using their vocabulary and knowledge of things of which she had no conscious awareness.[33] Jung was fascinated by this. He took down notes and later wrote his doctoral dissertation on these sessions, analyzing them psychologically from his newly acquired psychiatric perspective.[34] Helly was not named in the published document, but research later discovered her identity.

The sharply critical tone of the Zofingia lecture cited above demonstrates how angry Jung was that science would not take such experiences into account and study them as empirical data. Rationalistic psychology would not touch them. Jung felt this was based on blind prejudice. Standing in front of his fraternity brothers,

[33] S. Zumstein-Preiswerk, *C.G. Jung's Medium: Die Geschichte der Helly Preiswerk.*
[34] C.G. Jung, "On the Psychology and Pathology of So-Called Occult Phenomena."

he showed his famous temper. His lecture slammed the mistake of modern psychology for not considering this level of the mind, which he described as an intelligence exceeding time and space. As he had learned from his readings in philosophy (Schopenhauer, in particular), time and space are mental constructs based on the observation of material objects. In contrast, Jung quoted Kant several times as affirming the existence of the intelligence of the unconscious—what Jung would spend the rest of his life investigating.

In his studies of the inner world and the unconscious, Jung touched upon the world of religious and mythological thought, attracting strong criticism from the faculties on whose territory he was trespassing. This was the realm of the soul, the realm of the gods, the realm of spirits. Nevertheless, he considered this to be an aspect of the human psyche, and as a psychiatrist and psychotherapist, he referred to himself as a *Seelsorger*—a soul-keeper or caretaker. In his writings, the metaphysical and mythological became psychological.

Jung's interest in the occult also extended to an interest in parapsychology: telepathy, precognition, and extrasensory perception (ESP). He joined various associations for the study of parapsychology, including the Society for Psychical Research, founded in 1882, whose purpose was "to approach these varied problems without prejudice or prepossession of any kind, and in the same spirit of exact and unimpassioned enquiry which has enabled science to solve so many problems, once not less obscure nor less hotly debated."[35] This was exactly what Jung was advocating in his Zofingia lecture of 1897.

Jung's study of the unconscious also included the use of hypnosis in the early stages of his career as a psychoanalyst. Freud had used it, following in the footsteps of Jean-Martin Charcot and Pierre Janet, the French pioneers and masters of the art of hypnosis in the treatment of mental illness. Originally, this was called "mesmerism." Franz Anton Mesmer was an Austrian physician who used hypnosis to treat people with certain types of illnesses. Under hypnosis, they would speak of things that they did not know while they were in their ordinary state of ego-consciousness. Mesmerism and hypnosis point toward a territory in the human mind that is not available during ordinary waking consciousness. While Freud and Jung both used hypnosis at an early stage of their work as psychoanalysts, they later dropped

[35] Grattan-Guinness, I. *Psychical Research: A Guide to Its History, Principles and Practices: In Celebration of 100 Years of the Society for Psychical Research*, p. 19.

the practice because it did not have long-term curative effects. It could be used to penetrate that hidden part of the mind—the unconscious—and draw out certain thoughts and feelings, but these would quickly evaporate after the person became awake again and often could not recall what they had said or done while they were under the influence. In place of hypnosis, Freud developed a new method, based on what he called the "secret of dreams." By this, he was referring to the unconscious meanings that lay embedded but hidden in dreams, as they are remembered. Dreams must therefore be interpreted and stripped of their cover, so the secrets of the unconscious may be exposed.

When Jung entered his residency at the Burghölzli Clinic in 1900, Eugen Bleuler, his chief, asked him to review Freud's new book, *The Interpretation of Dreams*. Jung read it with great interest and was fascinated to see that Freud called the dream the "royal road to the unconscious." To follow this royal road to its destination in the unconscious, however, required psychological interpretation. The road might be royal, but it was also hidden by the defenders of the citadel to which it led. Freud had a specific method for removing these defenses and unveiling the meaning of dreams. His basic premise was that the purpose of dreaming was wish fulfillment. However, because the wish was unacceptable to ego-consciousness, its fulfillment in the dream was disguised. The task of the psychoanalytic interpreter was to unveil this secret and expose it to consciousness. Sometimes, this interpretation could cure the neurosis created by the repression of the wish, if the dreamer could accept the interpretation and bear it consciously. "Cure," here, means converting neurotic suffering into conscious suffering. For Jung, Freud's book confirmed his view that psychology and the psychiatric treatment of patients must consider the existence of the unconscious. This gave substance to his views about the importance of the unconscious for psychology and the value of understanding it for the treatment of neurosis and psychosis.

Another opportunity to study the unconscious opened for Jung when Prof. Bleuler asked him to do some empirical research using the "word association experiment" (WAE), a psychological test developed by the German psychologist Wilhelm Wundt. A team of residents at the Clinic was created with Jung as the leader. The WAE, as Jung inherited it, consisted of four hundred stimulus words, which for practical purposes he eventually reduced to one hundred. The stimulus words were spoken by the tester to a subject, while the tester noted the subject's verbal responses to each word and the time it took the subject to respond. Responses that were sufficiently faster or slower than the average response time across the set indicated a disturbance, otherwise labeled a "complex indicator." The cause of the disturbance would be emotional. Some words would disturb consciousness a great deal and produce several complex indicators, while others would disturb consciousness less or not at all. We might think of this like watching the surface of a pond when fish are feeding. If a fish makes a large ripple, one assumes it's a large fish; if it's a small ripple, it's a small fish. Eventually, Jung also attached a galvanometer to the arm of the subject to measure changes in the skin's conductivity while the test words were spoken. Sometimes the testers would also note other physiological changes, such as a headache, stomachache, or twitching. Jung and the other residents at the Clinic published their findings on the WAE in two volumes of *Diagnostische Associationsstudien*, as well as various psychiatric and neurological journals. The polygraph eventually evolved from their experiments.

From their findings, Jung developed his theory of complexes. He believed that the WAE was a scientific tool that could empirically discover an unconscious network of associations between a stimulus word and past experiences that had been largely repressed. Thus, it uncovered the affective remainder from traumatic experiences that were dissociated from consciousness and would not normally be reported during an anamnesis. In this research, Jung discovered that these forgotten or repressed experiences continued to have an active life in the unconscious, acting autonomously. They had a life of their own and contained an amount of free will or psychic energy. In that sense, they were akin to the ego complex. Jung concluded that the unconscious is populated by these split-off pieces of psyche, each with its own life. This concept of the "populated interior" became central to his understanding of the unconscious.

After Jung had completed this research using the WAE and formulated his theory of complexes, he turned his attention to mythology as an expression of the unconscious. Upon his return to Switzerland from his trip to America with Freud in 1909, he became deeply immersed in these studies and soon began writing *Transformations and Symbols of Libido* (first translated in 1916 as *The Psychology of the Unconscious*). This work would mark his departure from Freud's libido theory, which considered libido to be fundamentally sexual in nature and structured primarily by the Oedipus complex. In this work, Jung took a different approach and reformulated libido theory along the lines of the biological theory of vitalism as "psychic energy," without specific reference to sexuality. He analyzed a published account of fantasies by an American woman named

Frank Miller, which he found in an article published in Théodor Flournoy's journal, *Archives de Psychologie*. In this fantasy material he did not look for evidence of disguised or explicit sexual wish fulfillment, as Freud might have done. Instead, he found many parallels and common motifs in Miss Miller's material to what he had been reading about in Friedrich Creuzer's *The Symbolism and Mythology of Ancient Peoples* and other works. All these exotic references to symbolic imagery were totally unfamiliar to Miss Miller. This remarkable parallelism struck Jung as evidence of the existence of a level of psyche shared by all humans, which he would later call the "collective unconscious." This lower level of the psyche was thought to hold the images, motifs, and ideas that have occupied humanity since time immemorial—and continue to exist in modern times, as well.

In the opening chapter of *Transformations and Symbols of Libido*, Jung distinguished between two types of thinking: directed thinking and fantasy thinking. The latter consists of thinking with images that unfold in a non-rational or unplanned sequence. To a scientifically trained mind, this seems like a decidedly inferior type of thinking, which is how Jung spoke of it in this chapter of his book. But Jung would later reconsider this evaluation of fantasy thinking and appreciate its capacity to expose the unconscious. In fact, he became fascinated by imagination as a faculty offering an alternative way of thinking that is not inferior to directed thinking, but different.

After publishing his book and receiving dismissive reviews from Freud and others in his inner circle, Jung broke off personal and professional relations with these colleagues and underwent a period of profound self-questioning and introspection. As a part of his effort to sort out his new position with respect to psychoanalysis and the nature of the unconscious, he decided to experiment with the same type of mental activity that Miss Miller had engaged in—letting imagination have its way with consciousness to see what would appear. He called this an experiment, and it resulted in the creation of his fantastic *Red Book.*

Jung's experiment occupied him intensively from November 1913 through the summer of 1914, then intermittently through 1916. He carefully recorded the material obtained from his active imagination sessions in his journals (the *Black Books*), then created a transcript and a manuscript with interpretations, and finally produced what we now know as *The Red Book* (created between 1913 and 1928, but published only some fifty years after his death as *The Red Book: Liber Novus*).

During this period, imaginal figures appeared to Jung, revealing to him the landscape of the unconscious (the underworld) and instructing him in the meaning of symbols. Through this experience, he discovered the existence of an inner world that is continuously present in the unconscious, but noticed by consciousness only occasionally and indirectly. Active imagination became Jung's chief method for exploring the unconscious, replacing dreams as the "royal road to the unconscious." Using this method, Jung became an archeologist of the soul. His map of the soul is based largely on these experiences in imagination.

By opening his consciousness to the unconscious, Jung also gave voice to the "spirits of the dead" who lived there. This reminds us of his cousin Helly's mediumistic trances that gave voice to ancestral figures of the family, as well as his grandfather Samuel's conversations with his deceased wife. In Jung's experiences, however, the spirits spoke of their desperate need to find answers to questions left unanswered in their lifetimes and to find their way to a place of eternal rest. The answers were effectively delivered by the Gnostic teacher Basilides of Alexandria[36]

[36] C.G. Jung, *Memories, Dreams, Reflections*, pp. 378–390.

(or Philemon in *The Red Book*[37]) in the *Septem Sermones ad Mortuos* ("Seven Sermons to the Dead"). Thus were they released and could make their way to their homes among the stars. The unconscious has a claim upon consciousness, as Jung discovered, and consciousness has a duty to work with it for the sake of individuation. In his imagination, Jung conversed not with family figures, as his cousin Helly and his grandfather Samuel had done, but rather with historical figures such as Elijah and Salome, Philemon (aka Simon Magus, the Gnostic magician and philosopher), and Izdubar (aka Gilgamesh, the first recorded hero in Western history). This imaginal penetration into the deep cultural past connected his modern consciousness to sources of ancient wisdom and brought their wisdom to life in the present time. This was a work of deep cultural hermeneutics, interpreting ancient words of wisdom for modern times. Unlike his house dream, in which the lower levels were unpopulated, Jung's imaginal work revealed a richly peopled basement—a realm populated by autonomous figures, each with their own life and wisdom. Some of them represented the presence of instinct, such as the serpent accompanying

[37] C.G. Jung, *The Red Book: Liber Novus: A Reader's Edition*, pp. 508–535.

Salome; others represented spirit, such as Philemon the sage. With the dream of the multi-level house as a guiding image and the practice of active imagination as the lamp to illuminate the dark areas of the basements beneath the ground level, Jung surveyed the psyche's dimensions and inhabitants.

Following his *katabasis* (descent to the underworld), Jung began to develop theories that corresponded to his experiences, such as the theory of the archetypes of the collective unconscious and the Self. These were combined with his work on the theory of complexes and psychological typology to create what became the fundamentals of analytical psychology.

Levels of the Unconscious

When Jung mapped the unconscious, he showed its several layers or areas, as in the dream of the house with several basements. If one descends from the conscious level into the first area of the unconscious, there is what Jung designated as the personal unconscious. This first level below is somewhat accessible to consciousness and is experienced as the source of disturbances, as Jung discovered with the WAE. The inhabitants there are the unruly and autonomous feeling-toned "complexes," or sub-personalities, bound by association around an archetypal core. If provoked (or "triggered"), they generate emotions that disturb consciousness. Complexes that carry a lot of energy will disrupt consciousness to a major degree, even to the point of "possession" (psychotic break).

Jung investigated the origins of complexes and found the most frequent cause to be trauma—that is, a psychic experience that is sufficiently painful to warrant repression or dissociation. The traumatic experience is at first shocking, then painful, and then gradually (or sometimes quickly) put out of consciousness so the ego can function again and do its work of adjusting to the tasks at hand. Often, when people experience trauma, they seem to recover quickly—because they dissociate. This useful defense allows ego-consciousness to go on functioning in the moment. But the trauma is lodged in the psyche and forms part of a nucleus around which similar forgotten experiences can be attached. These "forgotten" experiences form a network of sensitive points in the unconscious. When the complex is triggered, it explodes into consciousness with strong affect, perseverates for a time, then gradually subsides when it has spent the energy contained within it. This dynamic sequence is what Jung explored with the WAE.

The existence of complexes is not cause for alarm or necessarily a call for treatment. Every person experiences traumas in early life and after. Typical traumas relate to family life. One speaks of a father complex or a mother complex because one's experiences with parents always contain traumatic events. This does not mean that parents severely traumatize the child intentionally, or even accidentally. Marcel Proust's kind mother did not come to say goodnight to him on one occasion, and he was traumatized for life and wrote about it at great length in his famous novel, *Remembrance of Things Past*. Parents who simply go about their business as adults, such as leaving the room suddenly for some reason or not arriving to school on time to pick up their youngster, may make a child suddenly feel abandoned and helpless and leave a scar for life. This may create or add to earlier traumas of a similar nature. When a parent punishes their child for some large or small misbehavior, they may traumatize the child momentarily and add energy and material to the complex. The Oedipus complex is one well-known result made famous by Freud in his theory of the super-ego. Also, accidents in childhood (which are inevitable) add to the material of a related complex. All these experiences contribute to the development of complexes in the lower level of the psyche beneath ego-consciousness.

Jung argued that, within complexes—including the parental complexes—there is an archetypal image, drawn from the deepest layer of consciousness. In the cases of the parental complexes, these are the archetypal images of the Great Mother and Great Father, which the child originally projects upon the parents. This archetypal projection accounts for the enormous and powerful impact parents have on their child's psyche. Parents, and especially the mother during the early stage of infancy, loom so large in the child's mind because children are totally dependent on them for care. Humans are born prematurely at nine months, and a lot of the physical development that takes place after birth in humans occurs before birth in other animals. Thus, the human infant is born in a highly precarious developmental condition and needs time, care, and nurture to continue developing—particularly neurologically—until it can begin to function in the human world, understand language, and assimilate cultural and social patterns of the group into which it is born. Parents are like gods to the young child, all-powerful and all-knowing. The core of the parental complexes, therefore, consists of a combination of a child's individual experiences of their human parents and the archetypal images of the Great Mother and Great Father that are projected onto them. The archetype gives the complex mass, strength, and energy, while the personal experiences give it individuality and specificity.

In addition to personal complexes in the lower floor of the psychic house, there are also cultural complexes. Following up on the classical work of Joseph Henderson (a first-generation Jungian analyst who, with colleagues, established the C.G. Jung Institute of San Francisco), Thomas Singer and Samuel Kimbles brought the concept strongly into the contemporary discussion in their book, *The Cultural Complex* (2004). While the concept has its original source in the writings of Jung, it has benefited from significant further development in the works of these later analysts.

There are basically two ways to consider the effects of the cultural complex: as a factor at play in the psyche of individuals and as a factor in the collective. On the individual side, cultural complexes are inherited from the culture in which a person grows up and lives, and they add further dimension to the complexes that have to do with family life and personal traumatic experiences. The cultural complex is a much broader category of complex than the personal. It is also based on trauma, which gets built into the culture of the collective—its symbols, religion, and rituals. Its effect is to influence and distort collective decisions and actions, just as personal complexes do to individuals. When a collective complex is triggered, it produces disturbances in collective feeling that lead to actions based on emotion, rather than rational thought. The collective ego, as represented by the collective's leadership at any given time, acts in accordance with the emotional atmosphere generated by the complex and the projections thrown onto "the other," who typically becomes representative of evil (via shadow projection). War is often the direct consequence of cultural complexes being triggered, as can be seen clearly in the events leading up to World Wars I and II, for example.

Cultures may experience trauma in various ways. For instance, a collective trauma may be caused by a natural event such as a devastating disaster (an earthquake, volcanic eruption, severe weather pattern that wipes out areas of a country's population, etc.). In such instances, God or the gods may be blamed and cursed, or prayed to for forgiveness and mercy. The cultural complex may also stem from human-made traumas such as war or abusive conflict among nations. When one nation goes to war against another and commits violent atrocities, destroys cities, and wreaks havoc on the population, it creates enduring trauma on a collective level. People who suffer from war, whether they are ultimately victorious or defeated, live with the effects of the trauma, because it becomes the core of a cultural complex. This complex is then passed down to subsequent generations through what is called the trans-generational transmission of trauma.

The effect on the individual of cultural complexes should not be confused with the effect of ordinary acculturation. Individuals are formed and shaped in many of their behaviors, attitudes, and feelings by the culture in which they grow up—they take on the habits of the culture, the language, the myths, the stories told about the nation's founding, and so forth. I grew up in the United States in the 1950s, and I heard many stories about the heroic figures who founded the nation. In elementary school, we recited the Pledge of Allegiance to the United States of America every morning: "… and to the Republic for which it stands, one nation, under God, indivisible, with liberty and justice for all." Messages like these take deep root in the psyche and create feelings of loyalty and attachment. One becomes nationalized, and the flag becomes a sacred symbol. This is not an expression of a cultural complex, however. It is based on the projection of an archetypal good parent, and it instills loyalty and attachment to the protective authorities. Traumatic events are different. They are memorialized with national holidays and celebrations, whose purpose is to remember them and convert them into events of history to be proud of and remembered. They are like funerals, which also function to decrease the trauma of death. Nevertheless, the complex created by the collective trauma is not eliminated by these rituals, and it can be used by leaders and political parties to excite the collective to become aggressive and charged up emotionally.

There are also stereotypical national characteristics, which are part of acculturation and perhaps the product of projection. Every nation has its typical character style, and as we grow up in these nations, we unconsciously assume features of this character by identification (*participation mystique*). We discover the extent of our national character when we go abroad and recognize how different we are from other national types—their attitudes, patterns of behavior, tastes, food, and language.

There is still another layer, or population, in the unconscious below the cultural level, and that is what Jung called the collective unconscious, or the "primitive" layer. This is the sub-basement of the psyche's house. Going down to this level in his dream, Jung discovered himself in a cave-like space with bones and prehistoric human skulls on the floor. There, he came upon the level of the psyche that is fundamental and universally common to all humans since time immemorial. All humans have features in their psyche that resemble all the others to some extent, because they have inherited archetypal patterns from this level. These features are often not identified by anthropologists, who tend to be more interested in social organization and cultural practices than in the deeper levels of the psyche. To get to this level, one must first get past the cultural differences in language, food, family structure, and one's relation to nature, and identify patterns of thought of a more abstract nature. The French anthropologist Claude Levy-Strauss took this approach in his explorations of structural features common to all human societies, as did Noam Chomsky in his study of the universal patterns in linguistics. What Jung wrote about concerning this most basic level of the psyche are the general patterns of human thought and behavior that are archetypal, and the common biologically-based sources and channels of energy, the instincts.

In Jung's psychological theory, instincts and archetypes join to form dynamic units that are energized by instinct and organized by archetypal patterns of thought and behavior into specific patterns: heroics, mating, mothering, creating, thinking and reflecting, and more. An instinct provides energy (libido), while an archetypal image provides direction and meaning. When this combination rises to the surface of consciousness and enters the space where the ego lives, it typically produces a strong emotional reaction that Jung called “numinous” (following Rudolf Otto, who described this experience as a *mysterium tremendum et fascinans*). A numinous experience takes consciousness beyond the level of a typical complex-charged emotional reaction into one felt to be divine, holy, transcendent, and larger than life. In ancient mythological times, there was a feeling of awe and respect in the presence of what were represented as sacred spaces (temples) and divinities (gods). In the modern and postmodern times, both buildings representing political power (the White House, the Kremlin, etc.) and celebrities (movie stars, dictators, astronauts, etc.) elicit a similar reaction, due to archetypal projections made on them by the media and the collective.

Today, it seems a curiosity that the gods could be worshiped in animal form (as a monkey, cat, sacred cow, etc.), as in ancient Egypt. Moses became apoplectic when he descended from Mount Sinai with the Tablets of Commandments to find that his people had built a golden calf and were worshipping it. They were not yet liberated from Egyptian habits of thought and feeling. The Greek gods were also represented by animal images—Athena by the owl, Apollo by the raven, Asclepius by the serpent and the dog. If we consider animals symbolic of instinct, then these sacred images join instinct and archetype together into meaningful and powerful personifications. Such personifications form the basis of all human religion and mythology. All the stories told in the mythological systems of the world are based on the archetypal patterns of the collective unconscious. What Jung did was compare the mythologies and find the commonalities.

When we look at the religious symbols that people hold up, honor, and worship, we see that they represent archetypal patterns of energy at a very high spiritual level, or a very embodied instinctual level. While people were once in awe of these symbols and worshipped them, in modern and post-modern societies, this reverence for representations of spiritual realities has more or less disappeared from the cultural horizon. Religions have fallen to a level of literalism and fundamentalism, or transformed themselves into ethical societies. Organized religions have not disappeared, but for many modern people they are antique ornaments on the tree of contemporary culture, and their magnificent structures have become museums. Their symbols do not speak to the soul of modern people and do not elicit the numinous response of days long ago. By science, they have been consigned to the category of vain images of fantasy and thrown into the dustbin of history as mere superstitions. Their metaphysical claims cannot be proven or tested in the laboratory, so they have no reality. In other cultures, and in earlier times in Western culture, the common sense of reality *included* archetypal and mythological dimensions.

Jung argued that while this mythical dimension has disappeared from collective consciousness (particularly in the West), it remains alive and active in the unconscious. In fact, the archetypal images previously represented publicly in temples and material images such as statues and paintings are more active in the unconscious than they were in the Middle Ages: earlier they were located and represented outside in churches and cathedrals, but now they are inside and agitate the psyche from within, like a complex. Moreover, modern people commonly project them onto celebrities and political leaders and messiahs, or onto ideologies that command faith and trust in their ideals, just as religious doctrines did in earlier times. Jung felt this presented modern people with a highly dangerous situation, because these projections carry such immense persuasiveness that people are swept up into belief systems and mental patterns that have little to do with reality and can easily lead to destructive attitudes and behavior when harnessed to mass-mindedness. In his essay "Wotan," he discussed such a "state of possession" (*Begriffenheit*) that German citizens were falling into at the time. It was 1936, just preceding the onset of World War II.[38]

Jung frequently stated that the unconscious is something alive, paradoxical, and mercurial. Mercurius, the alchemical symbol for the unconscious, is paradoxical in that he contains the opposites: "The Mercurius who personifies the unconscious is essentially 'duplex,' paradoxically dualistic by nature, fiend, monster, beast and at the same time panacea, 'the philosophers' son, *sapientia Dei*, and *donum spiritus Sancti*."[39] There are good elements in Mercurius—positive and creative movements and directions—and there are nasty, bad, evil ones. Both are contained within the spirit of the unconscious. Jung had great respect for the unconscious, and was not in the least naive about this force of nature. He knew that unconscious powers can assist us, and also destroy us. All depends on what kind of relation we have to it. The ego's relationship to the unconscious is all-important for psychic health and maturity.

[38] C.G. Jung, "Wotan," CW 10, para. 386.

[39] C.G. Jung, "The Psychology of the Transference," para. 389.

Chapter Three

Persona, Shadow, Anima and Animus

In this chapter, I will speak about several quite well-known and frequently referenced Jungian features of the psychological makeup of the individual: the persona, the shadow, the anima, and the animus. While these terms are quite familiar to many cultured people today, they remain to be considered as deep psychological realities, and significant figures occupying the deeper levels of the house in which the ego complex occupies the first floor.

Persona

Persona, a Latin word from Roman theater meaning "mask," was adopted by Jung to speak of an archetypal feature of the personality. Originally, the persona referred to the mask actors wore on stage to perform roles assigned to them in the play. With the mask in place, a male actor could play any role, including a *femme fatale*. The actor could also change masks and thereby assume several roles in the play. His character would be determined and clearly shown by the face painted onto the front of the mask. If he put on a mask of Oedipus and stepped on stage, he would become that character, speak his lines, accept his fate, and receive applause for his theatrical performance. When leaving the stage, he would put on his street clothes, step out of the theater, and play the role he assumed in his personal life—son, father, husband, lover, student, and so forth. He would no longer be wearing an actor's mask, but he would still be operating with a persona in the psychological sense. The persona is always a representation of a common (i.e., archetypal) figure. This is what gives it value and makes it easily identifiable to the "audience"—that is, to those who perceive the image on the face of the personality. They can relate to the wearer because their apperceptive function responds with familiarity and feeling. Is he a hero? Is she a siren? The persona provides a clue, but it also hides the face behind the mask.

When the K-Pop group, BTS, first picked up my book, *Jung's Map of the Soul*, and began creating albums based on Jungian concepts, the first song they chose to perform was titled *Persona*. I suspect this was because they were suffering from celebrity—the result of a persona eliciting mass public projections. Archetypal images were identified with the performers playing a role on stage, and those performers felt the pressure to live up to those projections, even when not onstage, but merely in public. Celebrities are always self-conscious on stage. This is the burden they bear for their success. BTS sang about this phenomenon and essentially told their fans that what they saw on stage was a persona, and did not match their individual personalities off stage. Their songs were psychologically instructive and reached a wide audience throughout the world.

In the theater, the persona of the actor is a temporary identity assumed for the purpose of the performance, while off stage, the persona is an enduring, consistent manner of self-presentation for the purpose of relating to others in society. Persona is a constant feature of the personality—always present—because one is onstage in all of life, from childhood to adulthood to old age and death. There is even the "death mask" of the famous. As Jacque, the rather cynical character in Shakespeare's play *As You Like It,* muses: "All the world's a stage, / and all the men and women merely players." He continues to enumerate the seven stages of a man's life: infant, scholar, lover, soldier, rotund mature adult, shrunken old man, and finally ancient dodderer, "sans teeth, sans eyes, sans taste, sans everything." The truth is, one is constantly onstage in life, although the persona changes with age. It is sometimes called "the face we wear to meet the other faces." All of these faces are grounded in archetypal images. The cosmetics and fashion industries know this well, and help customers create and sustain a recognizable persona.

If someone is asked to submit a *curriculum vitae* for some professional purpose—like applying for a job or submitting a paper to a journal for publication—what is put in the document is a description of a suitable persona for the purpose. The same is done when filling out a dating profile for online search engines that will elicit a response from potential mates. One dresses up to go to the opera or to dine where a dress code is implicitly or explicitly specified. People find it awkward to be caught by surprise when the doorbell rings and they are not prepared to meet the caller, because they are momentarily without their normal persona. In dreams about clothing, the interpretation generally tends toward persona issues in the dreamer's life.

A person develops their persona in a very natural way. From the beginning of life, humans observe others and imitate them. Then they await a reaction. The mother smiles at the baby, and the baby smiles back. Both are happy. This seems to happen instinctually and is instilled in the psyche by the need to be accepted and loved. It is human nature written into the codes that govern spontaneous behavior, and it has survival value because the environment responds. Children who grow up with animals adopt a persona that is consistent with the animals around them. By imitating those animals, they adapt to their expectations and join the pack. This imitative behavior forms bonds of kinship and respect. Over time, a consistent sense of identity based on this internalized behavior pattern becomes a familiar part of the personality. One feels at home with a specific group of people and alien in another. Some would consider the persona a "false self," but this is true only if there is no greater awareness of selfhood than what is presented in the persona. There is a person behind the mask who is not identical with it. To some extent, one must be false to certain parts of the self in order to participate in a group and maintain an atmosphere of social conviviality. Some people have an extremely attractive persona, and everyone they meet wants to be their friend. Others have the opposite effect on others, and people shun them. Who is hiding the most? To answer, one must know the person wearing the mask. The mask reveals and the mask conceals. In the psychoanalytic relationship, the persona falls away after a time, and the naked person is revealed. This is considered the beginning of the individuation process in analysis. However, analysis is not meant to be a social setting in which one gets along over a cup of tea. It is more penetrating, like a surgical theater. Clothes off. For people unaccustomed to this degree of psychic intimacy, it comes as a shock.

This is not to say that the persona should be put aside in other contexts. It is extremely valuable for social and political or diplomatic interactions. Imagine people speaking their spontaneous thoughts and feelings in a classroom or at a party or at the office. It would bring social intercourse to a halt and cause consternation and confusion. Within families, this often happens around the dinner table because people feel free "to be themselves." The persona is left at the door and one's more natural self feels liberated to say things and behave in a way that one would not in a public space. It is common for children to go to school and be very well-behaved with teachers and friends, but come home and be absolute brats in front of their parents.

Some people, on the other hand, identify with their public role and persona to such an extent that they never lay it aside. In these cases, ego-consciousness is totally identified with the public persona. The senator comes home to his family in his three-piece suit, and his wife addresses him as senator in front of the children. His children then follow the lead of their mother and address him as senator, and later that night his mistress addresses him as senator. Everybody calls him senator, and he accepts this and behaves like a senator wherever he goes. This is a problem of identification with the persona: it becomes the "I" in a deep and exclusive sense and blocks further individuation.

When one becomes conscious that one has a persona and can recognize what it looks like, one is confronted with the question: Well, what else am I? A period of self-examination then ensues that can lead to greater consciousness. The first realization comes in the form of the shadow.

Shadow

What lies behind the mask? The shadow is usually the first of the figures who appears when the door is opened to the unconscious. Faust finds a little poodle dog on his walk and brings him home, where the animal morphs into Mephisto. At first, the shadow appears as something that is a bit other—"not-I"—as something surprising, alien, and even monstrous. On one level of the basement, it is only what the social context rejects as not suitable. These are features of thought, feeling, motivation, and potential behavior that are not acceptable to be shown in social life, and must be hidden to get along. To some extent, these features of the personality are conscious, in the sense that one is aware of holding them in check.

But to a larger extent, they are unconscious because they are repressed. The more conscious features would be what you feel about someone and do not say to them. You might smile politely while feeling and thinking that you don't like this person, or that you would be very critical of them if you told them what you really thought about what they're saying, and doing, and how they look, and how they're dressed. So, you keep those thoughts to yourself. But at a deeper level is the question of projection. What of your shadow are you projecting onto others? This reaches down into the archetypal dimension.

For the purpose of becoming more conscious, value is placed on looking the shadow in the face. Some features of the shadow, however, are very difficult to hold in consciousness because they provoke instant and outright rejection. Ego defenses shut out shadow realizations because they are painful or frightening. One should not think or feel this way! For instance, the problem of envy is a difficult one to admit into consciousness because of the shame of having to admit it. It can be about fame and glamour, about wealth, about beauty, about talent, about power. Many attractors summon an envy response. The feeling is uncomfortable and usually hidden from consciousness, even as one engages in attacking the attractor with subtle innuendoes and undermining enactments. The feelings that we hide from ourselves remain unconscious but make noises in the basement and often appear in dreams.

Freud discovered this phenomenon in his own dreams. In his famous interpretation of "Irma's injection" dream, he uncovered his own hidden feelings of shame and guilt and his need to be seen as innocent and clean. Jung admired Freud for his courage in facing the shadow in himself and exposing it in his psychoanalytic writings. Viennese culture was famous for its polite formalities and equally for its blatant hypocrisy. Many poets and artists expressed this comically and tragically in their works, and Freud did the same in his psychoanalytic essays and books. In *The Interpretation of Dreams,* he showed how the division between ego-consciousness and the shadow operates. The latent dream content, which is the "real dream" and expresses the hidden wishes of the shadow personality, is denied entry into the manifest dream content by the censor, a kind of policeman at the door. A subtle mechanism called "dream work" allows for a carefully disguised version of the shadow to enter the manifest dream by rendering it acceptable through an elaborate program of symbolization, displacement, and deceptive elaboration. The task of the dream interpreter is to undo what dream work has accomplished and expose the truth of the unconscious wish. The wish is shameful to the persona-identified ego-consciousness. Freud's open discussion of such shadow material made him a pariah in Vienna's social circles, as well as among psychiatrists throughout Europe. Jung, however, admired Freud for his boldness and championed him at home and abroad. Freud focused particularly on the wish for incestuous sexual relations, which are expressed indirectly and in disguise in social contexts and uncovered in psychoanalysis. Jung picked up the theme of incest in his essay "The Psychology of the Transference," many years after his break with Freud.

The repression of shadow material amounts to instinctive avoidance of painful thoughts and feelings (e.g., guilt, shame) and socially and ethically unacceptable desires. Avoidance of shame is evident from early in life. In fact, much of the socialization process is based on shaming children into conformity, from toilet-training to enforcing correct manners at the dinner table and on the playground. A shameless person may be secretly admired for their lack of ordinary inhibitions, but will be shunned by the majority. Sociopathy and psychopathy are defined as the absence of shame and guilt for breaches in lawful conduct and represent the manifestation of the shadow in society.

The normal defenses of the ego push asocial impulses underground into the unconscious through the mechanisms of suppression, which is conscious, and repression, which is unconscious. Either way, the process is one of dissociation. The innocent ego lives on the first floor of the house and the shadow lives in the basement. And the rule is that what is in the unconscious gets projected onto others. Thus, if envy is unconscious, it will be projected onto other people, and the subject will see them as envious of oneself or of others. If aggression is repressed, it will be projected onto others who will be seen as aggressive, while the subject remains an innocent victim. Aggressive enactments will be done unconsciously and denied. This is a picture of the shadow at work in society at all levels.

How does the individual discover and take responsibility for their personal shadow? One way is to analyze projections. The rule in Jungian work is that if one has a strong negative emotional reaction to someone, ask: Where is that in them? Where is that feature they find so disgusting or disgraceful in themself? This is very difficult work. It is what we see Freud doing in his interpretation of his dreams, unveiling the shadow within himself.

Erich Neumann developed this theme of shadow analysis in *Depth Psychology and a New Ethic*. He argued that the "old ethic" applies the law externally, while the "new ethic," based on shadow analysis, applies the law inwardly. The old ethic is based on following the rules laid down by the priests and judges and developing a respectable persona, thereby remaining righteous and seemingly innocent. Shadow is projected outward onto "the other." All the denied sins (shadow effects) of the community are placed on the scapegoat, who is driven into the wilderness. This cleanses the community, allowing it to go on in the old ways. The community gains relief from the symptoms of sinfulness, but the underlying cause remains untreated. Thus, the ritual needs to be repeated regularly to insure the community's self-righteousness.

The new ethic, based on depth psychology, requires self-examination before one judges others with projected images. The question must be asked: How am I contributing to this harmful behavior? After that question is sincerely answered, remedial action is called for to stop the subject's role in the situation and set up a more conscious framework for future relations. The subject takes responsibility insofar as unconscious shadow enactments have created a situation that fosters misdeeds on the part of the other. Neumann wrote this profound work while living in Tel Aviv in the 1940s. It contains deep insight into the ways in which individuals and groups interact to generate hatred and mistrust, which in turn lead to violence and an attempt to exterminate the evil other, who is made into a scapegoat. Neumann saw this happening in Nazi Germany to the Jews, and in Palestine to the indigenous population.

The deep and painful self-examination Neumann called for constitutes his "new ethic," in which the judgment of others (or of oneself) is not abolished or deleted, but occurs after careful self-examination, which is then considered in the judgment of the other. One may still defend oneself from the other's aggression, but in a way that considers one's own role in creating their aggressive acts. Such reflection and consideration has the opportunity to create a new situation whereby the aggression is not repeated. However, this requires taking responsibility for the shadow. This is not easy and is not often done. As Jung wrote—very realistically:

> While some traits peculiar to the shadow can be recognized without too much difficulty as one's own personal qualities, in this case [of projections] both insight and good will are unavailing because the cause of the emotion appears to lie, beyond all possibility of doubt, in the *other person.* No matter how obvious it may be to the neutral observer that it is a

> matter of projections, there is little hope that the subject will perceive this himself.[40]

Jung described the shadow as an autonomous complex, like a mythological demon who, along with the other archetypes of the collective unconscious, was "there from the beginning." This biblical view of the shadow places it already active in the Garden of Eden, as the serpent who tempts Eve to disobey the Father Creator, and again in the second generation as the evil waiting at the flap of Cain's tent to take possession of him and direct him to murder his brother.[41] The rather shallow levels of shadow, such as one's less than acceptable thoughts, feelings, fantasies, and attitudes, are relatively easy to become conscious of, but the thing-itself, the archetypal core of the complex, is as elusive as Mercurius. There is a level of shadow as deep as the bottom of the Inferno, and very few people encounter it or become aware of it. This is what Jung called "absolute evil."

Absolute evil is represented in fairytales, in religion, and in the world's mythologies. Jung came upon it several times in *Liber Novus*, during his exploration of

---

[40] C.G. Jung, *Aion*, para. 16. Italics in the original.
[41] Genesis 4:7.

the archetypal unconscious. In Dante's *Divine Comedy*, Part I, *Inferno*, there are many circles of Hell, and at each level Dante confronts sinners of a certain type—the lascivious, the gluttons, the thieves, and so forth. These are souls who are not willing to work on themselves, not willing to realize their shadow aspects and make amends. They insist on their right to continue doing what they have been doing all their lives, even while they are suffering for it in Hell. Because they are not willing to confess and engage in the arduous process of passing through Purgatory, they remain in Hell. The crimes and punishments get worse as Dante descends into the cold and darkness of the sunless Inferno. At the very bottom of Hell, he sees the frightful figure of Dis—Satan—locked in ice from the waist down, his bat-like wings flapping to maintain the freezing cold, and chewing on three hapless corpses in the mouths of his three heads. This is a poetic representation of absolute evil. As Jung wrote: "It is quite within the bounds of possibility for a man to recognize the relative evil of his nature, but it is a rare and shattering experience for him to gaze into the face of absolute evil."[42] Dante nearly faints when he gazes on the figure of Satan.

[42] C.G. Jung, *Aion*, para. 19.

Jung's strong insistence that the shadow has an archetypal core and is active in human affairs, whether recognized or not, found strong expression in his controversy about the nature of evil with Fr. Victor White. The Dominican priest maintained the Roman Catholic theological view that evil is to be defined philosophically, as the absence of good (*privatio boni*), and did not have any being beyond that. This would be a naturalistic view of the nature of shadow as the absence of light behind an object that is blocking the light from shining in that space. Jung became furious with this view, because it did not consider the power and autonomy of evil as a force. His view of the shadow's reality was more in line with mythological and biblical accounts. In this sense, Jung respected myth above rational philosophy and theology and felt it closer to what is experienced psychologically and empirically. "Evil is not an absence," he could be heard shouting. "It is a power, and it must not be underrated!"

This very dark aspect of the psyche manifests in a type of egocentrism or egoism that is utterly cold and without empathy for anything or anyone else. It has one purpose: to dominate. It cares for nothing but power over others. One runs from it when one sees it because it is so chilling to be close to such cold-blooded evil. Mostly it is subtle, like the wily serpent in Paradise, pretending to assist in raising consciousness and spiritual awareness—"Eat of this and you will wise like the Father, knowing good from evil." Other exemplars of the shadow are more blatant. Forensic psychologists have interviewed rapists and killers in prisons, and they describe the inner life of the psychopaths as cold, without remorse, guilt, or shame for whatever atrocities they have committed. Referring to childhood, these psychopaths would claim they had been "dissed," meaning not seen, heard, or respected. Often early traumas would be concealed and long-forgotten. They would speak like Cain, who felt humiliated by the Lord's preference for his brother Abel's offering. They would do it again if they were released, and they would be utterly incorrigible. Such psychopaths are possessed by the archetypal shadow. They bear the mark of Cain. In their case, it is on full display. One can learn from both kinds of shadow representation—the subtle and the blatant.

Anima and Animus

Along with the shadow as an archetypal figure, Jung also wrote about the anima and animus as having the same level of psychological reality. They contribute to the "not-I" part of the personality, which Jung located in the basement of the house of the psyche.

Anima is a Latin word meaning "soul," while *animus* is Latin for "spirit." Thus, the anima and animus are foreigners to the conscious mind. They are distinctly *other*. The shadow resembles more closely the identity of the ego-conscious mind, personified as being of the same gender. The anima and animus, however, have a more distant relationship to the identity of the conscious mind, being of the other gender.

In Jung's experience and exposition, the anima is personified as a feminine figure, and the animus as a masculine figure, hence the difference in their titles. In Latin, words ending in *-a* indicate the feminine gender, and words ending in *-us* indicate the masculine gender. Thus, the anima archetype is feminine and a content of the collective unconscious in men, while the animus archetype is masculine and a content of the collective unconscious in women. According to the law of projection, whatever is unconscious is projected onto objects in the environment. Therefore, men project the anima onto women, and women project the animus onto men. The psychological results are similar, in that both projections create an overwhelming surge of longing for and symbolic magnification of the other. A woman enhanced by an anima projection is a goddess or dangerous siren, while the animus-enhanced man is a god or devil. On the inner level, the anima bestows life itself, energy, hope, and love in a man feeling her presence, and the animus bestows meaning, spirituality, and wisdom to the ego-consciousness of a woman experiencing this archetypal complex. Jung wrote of the animus as a psychopomp—a guide of souls to the higher realms of spirit.[43]

In Jung's late work *Aion*, there is a chapter titled "The Syzygy: Anima and Animus." This indicates their close, almost twin-like relationship. In the Pleroma stage at the beginning of individuation, they form a single complex, as in the Platonic myth of the original man-woman being at the beginning of human life. (The Platonic myth describes three original beings, each made up of two-in-one: a male-female, a male-male, and a female-female. At a certain point in time, these pairs were divided, and the male-female pair became man and woman, the male-male pair two men, and the female-female pair two women.[44]) Separated, they search for the missing other with great longing and desire to find their original soulmate. When they succeed, they form a couple, both physically and psychologically—a loving pair of soulmates: "So ancient is the desire of

[43] C.G. Jung, *Aion*, para. 33.
[44] Plato, "Symposium," *The Portable Plato*, pp. 143ff.

one another which is implanted in us, reuniting our original nature, making one of two, and healing the state of man."[45] This is the story of individuation, regarding the integration of ego-consciousness and the archetypal energies personified by the anima and animus.

Typically, and according to tradition, a person in the first half of life consolidates their ego identity around the part of the syzygy that corresponds to their biological sex. People who are born female identify with the feminine part of the syzygy and become mature exemplars of the feminine by midlife, and people born male identify with the masculine part of the syzygy and become mature exemplars of the masculine. The born female becomes feminine, and the born male becomes masculine. The masculine part of the syzygy that is left behind in a woman's development is the animus, and this is projected onto a man who matches it. For the man, it is the other way round, and he projects the feminine anima onto a woman. In this way, they form a couple and procreate. This is the program laid down by the codes of nature, and they serve the viability of the species. In the second half of life, a counter movement sets in. Rather than repressing the opposite (as one has

[45] Ibid., p. 146.

done in the first half) and looking for it outside oneself, one begins to discover it within. By midlife, women have given birth and nurtured their children, and begin to study and write books. Men have studied and written books, and begin to cook in the kitchen and nourish relationships. This is the cartoon version of the shift, but it communicates the basic idea of the transformation that takes place at midlife. Integration of the opposites previously separated by the *principium individuationis* begins to occur at the conscious level and the result is psychological androgyny. This is the second stage of the lifelong individuation process.

When Jung wrote about the anima and animus, he had something like this in mind. At the beginning of life, in infancy, there is no psychological distinction between genders, even though there is a physical difference. The psychological distinction arrives later, as a result of the *principium individuationis.* The child becomes aware of the world around and the difference between mama and papa, between herself and her brother, between himself and his girlfriends at school. This signals separation in the syzygy. The child's ego identifies with one of the two parts of the syzygy, and this enters its persona and self-identity. The other part falls away and remains in the unconscious. The figure that is not identified with is projected onto mother or father, and later onto a person who matches the unconscious love object, who is often referred to as a "soulmate."

When there is a significant match between one's anima or animus complex and an outer person, ego-consciousness experiences infatuation. This is an illusion from an objective point of view, but on the inner level it is a profound meeting with the lost other of the syzygy, with whom union promises blissful wholeness, perfection, and eternal life. This is due to the archetypal quality of the experience, which renders it numinous in the strong sense of the word—a *mysterium tremendum et fascinans*, as Rudolf Otto defined it.[46] The anima and animus come trailing clouds of glory. As Jung would say, "the Goddess herself descends into them and conjures up an ineffable springtime,"[47] and the witnessing ego must honor and worship Her, helpless to do otherwise. The other in this situation is perceived as archetypal—as more than human, even divine. Even die-hard atheists are convinced of the reality of the transcendent when "She Who Must Be Obeyed"[48] shows up in their lives. This encounter becomes the story of love-and-marriage,

[46] R. Otto, *The Idea of the Holy.*

[47] A. Schweizer (ed.), *C.G. Jung Letters to Hedy Wyss*, p. 26.

[48] Title of a novel by Rider Haggard—a favorite of Jung's to illustrate the power of the anima.

as told in many fairytales. Mild forms of the anima or animus experience take place early in life, such as in childhood infatuations and adolescent romances, but its strongest form typically appears at midlife or after. At that point, the other loves seem childish and superficial. A fully developed ego-consciousness is prepared for the archetypal experience, while earlier stages were not.

Nowadays, the psychological situation seems somewhat different, because often young people do not make this sharp and absolute distinction between masculine and feminine, either in themselves or in the world around them. For them, the syzygy tends to remain less divided, and the *principium individuationis* is not as decisive in making the distinction between masculine and feminine as it was in traditional times and societies. This may be an effect of Mother Nature trying to reduce overpopulation on the planet, as Marie-Louise von Franz predicted would happen fifty years ago.[49]

While Jung wrote about the anima often and in various ways, he wrote far less frequently about the animus. Perhaps his most succinct definition of these

[49] Heard in a lecture at the C.G. Jung Institute Zurich in the early 1970s.

archetypes is captured in the phrases, "the archetype of life itself" for the anima and "the archetype of meaning" for the animus.[50] The anima is soul—the conduit of psychic energy from the Self to the ego. Often the anima is associated with Eros, the god of love, whose sharp arrows pierce the heart of the lover and bring hot pangs of desire and longing for his beloved, who now embodies the goddess. This story is told in countless works of art—by poets such as the author of the biblical Song of Songs, as well as Dante, Shakespeare, and Pushkin, and by composers such as Richard Wagner, in his classic rendition of the magical transformation that overtakes the surprised couple in his opera, *Tristan und Isolde*. It is the eternal story of high passion. Jung's perception of Freud was that he was in the grip of the anima when he spoke of sexuality:

> for Freud, sexuality was undoubtedly a *numinosum*... Basically, he wanted to teach... that, regarded from within, sexuality included spirituality and had an intrinsic meaning... Perhaps some inner experience of his might

[50] C.G. Jung, "Archetypes of the Collective Unconscious," para. 66.

> have opened his eyes but then his intellect would have reduced any such experience to 'mere sexuality' of 'psychosexuality.' He remained the victim of the one aspect he could recognize and for that reason I see him as a tragic figure for he was a great man and what is more, a man in the grip of his daimon.[51]

In his conceptions of the anima and animus as archetypes, Jung included sexuality and spirituality within the experience of Eros for a man, and sexuality and transcendent spirituality in the experience of intimate relationship for a woman. Animus is associated with logos ("the word"), which brings to consciousness profound thoughts that confer an extraordinary depth of transcendent meaning to the love experience. With anima and animus together, the love experience becomes an experience of "life itself" and "transcendent meaning"—the divine Syzygy realized on a conscious level. When this happens, the house of psyche is brightly lit and set on the mountaintops. Across all cultures, the wedding celebration is an attempt to capture this vision.

[51] C.G. Jung, *Memories, Dreams, Reflections*, pp. 252–253.

At the inner level, this is also a union with the anima or animus within, which reaches to the deepest levels of the collective unconscious. Now, anima and animus become a link between the ego and the Self. This is what Jung discovered in his active imagination journey at midlife. The feminine figure he met in his *Red Book* experience was named Soul, and she taught him about her autonomy and transcendence. With her accompaniment, Jung discovered his inner world, which was replete with figures like Elijah the prophet and Philemon the Gnostic teacher. And it was Soul who brought him the gift from heaven—a crown with the inscription, "Love never ends."[52] These were wisdom figures, beyond time and space, representations of the Self.

[52] C.G. Jung, *The Red Book: Liber Novus: Reader's Edition*, p. 441.

Chapter Four

Psychic Energy

The psyche is a system in motion. There are structures, as I described in the previous chapters, but those structures are not static. They are in constant movement in relation to one another. The psyche is a dynamic system operating on a given supply of energy. What is the source of psychic energy? And how is it directed and channeled in the psyche?

Both Jung and Freud inherited a notion of psychic energy from the German philosophical tradition, notably from the philosopher Arthur Schopenhauer. In his major work, *The World as Will and Representation*, Schopenhauer postulated that the energy behind all that exists on the manifest level of existence is what he called "the Will." The Will is blind to moral distinctions or cultural habits and inhibitions. It is simply a force that wants expression in existence and is responsible for all natural objects, both organic and inorganic. Human beings, as creatures of nature, are a result of the Will's desire to be and are subject to the directives of the Will. As physical beings, they conform to the blind Will in many ways—some healthy and some neurotic. The Will compels them to stay alive at all costs. Thus, it is healthy to take care of one's body and physical wellbeing; however, this can become a neurotic obsession. As a means of deliverance from the Will and the illusions it creates in the mind, Schopenhauer was drawn to the recently translated *Upanishads* and their teaching that our picture of the world is illusory. Inspired by these texts, he thought that slavery to the desires of the Will could be overcome (i.e., channeled and sublimated) through concentrated mental activities such as meditation and contemplation, if the conscious mind was sufficiently determined and trained. Jung followed this line of thought to a point, but took a different view of the Will as an expression of the Self with a meaningful goal—namely wholeness, and not merely existence for its own sake.

Nietzsche picked up Schopenhauer's notion of the Will and brought it to expression in his famous "will to power." The *Übermensch* ("superior person") that Nietzsche imagined in his writings was one who had conquered all psychological conflicts and conditionings and identified with the will to power, which he described as self-overcoming. The overcoming required was a type of sublimation of the more primitive will to live, resulting in radical self-determination. Both Schopenhauer and Nietzsche have been criticized by many thinkers for suggesting that the will to power is the answer. According to these critics, it is not the answer, but in fact the problem, as it leads to ego-centrism and ego-inflation. Jung would refer to this state as the "mana personality" and emphasize its danger from a psychiatric and psychological viewpoint. In his extended seminar on Nietzsche's *Zarathustra*, he held up Nietzsche's life as an example of the descent into psychosis.

Freud's libido theory echoes Schopenhauer's notion of the Will, as the libido is thought to be the fundamental source of psychic energy. When Thomas Mann first read Freud after having studied Schopenhauer for many years, he said he could hardly tell the difference between their theories. Both were pessimistic about the possibility for humans to overcome either the Will (for Schopenhauer) or sexual desire and the pleasure principle (for Freud, comprising part of the Id). Both theories asserted that most—if not all—humans were trapped by the power of the Will or sexual desire, and could not (and did not) want to overcome it. They were guided blindly and thus victims of the Will or the Id.

In Freud's biologically-based thinking, the sexual instinct provides the energy for the psychic system. This is why he termed psychic energy "libido," using the Latin word for "desire" or "lust." If sexual energy is blocked from fulfilling its wish in orgasm, there are several possible outcomes—principally, sublimation and neurosis. Through sublimation (i.e., finding a substitute expression), libido can be used to create culture. Jung joked about this: "What one usually understands by sublimation is only a repression: say there is some sex fantasy – one represses it and plays the piano instead."[53] Sublimation of sexuality in cultural activity is a poor substitute for sexual pleasure with an ideal partner. Thus, Freud felt that sublimation was not necessarily a total failure in this respect, but it was not completely satisfactory from the libido's point of view. In *Civilization and Its Discontents,* he wrote about the malaise that results in civilized life because, even at its best, the pleasures of culture do not fully satisfy the instinct. Nevertheless, it is better than the other possibility, which is neurosis. If sexuality cannot be lived and satisfied in the way it wishes, or at least moderately satisfied through sublimation, the psyche

[53] C.G. Jung, *Visions*, vol. 1, p. 293.

rebels and creates a neurotic conflict. Freud's treatment for psychoneurosis (and hysteria, in particular) was to analyze the blockage and try to allow for some freedom, so the patient could become conscious of what the sexual desire was and wanted, and to some extent live that. He did not recommend total sexual freedom, as was later advocated by some of his followers. These included proponents of radical liberation from all restraints on the instinct, such as Wilhelm Reich, who argued that political repression and fascism are rooted in sexual repression and should therefore be abolished for the sake of social justice. Sexual freedom would result in a free and healthy society, he believed.

For a time, Jung agreed with Freud's view of the etiology of psychoneurosis. When he was training as a psychiatrist at the Burghölzli Clinic and following Freud's thinking, he used that point of view to treat some patients. He concluded rather quickly that not all mental illness is the result of the repression of sexuality. There are other factors involved and other psychological causes of mental illnesses such as schizophrenia. He also regarded culture as an authentic creation of the human mind and not attributable to the sublimation of the sexual instinct. As he separated himself from his projection of "the master" onto Freud, he began to think about libido as psychic energy in a non-sexual sense. He later spoke of "a dynamic or creative principle which I have termed libido"[54] and proceeded to argue that psychic energy (libido) can be channeled into various areas of human activity without losing the benefit of full satisfaction. The other-than-sexual areas into which psychic energy may be channeled are not substitutes or replacements for sexual libido, but have their own distinct goals and methods for achieving full gratification. There is no remaining discontent due to absence of orgasm. In his breakaway book from Freud, *Wandlungen und Symbole der Libido*, Jung wrote of "symbols of transformation" that produce natural canalizations of psychic energy through a process of "psychization." It would take him a great deal of further reflection and experience to free himself entirely from Freud's mono-instinct view of libido and to develop his broader conception of psychic energy as multi-instinctual.

Progression and Regression of Psychic Energy

Before looking at the variety of instinctual sources that Jung listed as features in the distribution of psychic

[54] C.G. Jung, *Psychological Types*, para. 336.

energy, I will first discuss his view of the mechanics of psychic energy's flow. In an essay titled "On Psychic Energy," written some fifteen years after his break with Freud over the understanding of libido, Jung described two basic directions in the flow of psychic energy: progressive and regressive.[55] When psychic energy is flowing progressively, it is moving from its source in the unconscious into daily life: toward love and work, relationships of all kinds, hobbies and interests. To Jung, energy meant interest. Thus, to have libido for something means to take an interest in it. With libido progression, there follows a general sense of satisfaction with life as it proceeds from day to day. As long as there are no serious blockades, beyond a few slow-downs or bumps in the road, life is good. The American psychologist Mihaly Csikszentmihalyi, in his book *Flow*, describes the progression of psychic energy as bringing a feeling of being totally at one with one's activities. However, lesser degrees of progression are also evident in a daily life that one regards as reasonably meaningful.

The opposite movement of psychic energy is termed "regression," which occurs when progression is blocked by obstacles—be these inner (such as neurotic

[55] C.G. Jung, "On Psychic Energy," para. 60ff.

conflicts) or outer (such as relationship breakdowns, career setbacks, illnesses, or deaths of loved ones). In these moments, ego-consciousness registers the feeling of being depressed or stuck, unable to summon the energy to continue one's daily business with any degree of interest or satisfaction. This is sometimes referred to as "burnout," or more seriously as "break-down" or clinical depression. There is little energy for life, and what remains is used grudgingly. One becomes a miser of energy and withdraws from active life.

But energy does not disappear or simply evaporate. Rather, Jung argued for the conservation of energy along the lines of how energy is considered in physics, arguing that it does not disappear but flows back into the unconscious from whence it came, and is thus unavailable to ego-consciousness. In the movement of regression, the river goes in the opposite direction from its usual flow. It empties itself into the dark hole of the unconscious and runs underground. This is the image Jung found in his first active imagination after his break with Freud: an underground river with the corpse of a youth with blond hair and a wound to the head floating in it.[56] Jung said he was in a "state of dissociation" at the

[56] C.G. Jung, *Memories, Dreams, Reflections*, p. 179.

time and "suspended in mid-air."[57] The psychic energy normally available for life had gone underground.

When a regression happens, the unconscious is activated. This may result in strong and impressive symbolic dreams and visions. At these times, active imagination is easier to engage in than during periods when libido is progressing strongly into the tasks of daily life. For this reason, artists often report that it is during these fallow times in their lives that inspiration for the next project comes to them. One may lack the energy to act on the images that appear, but one can hold them in mind and contemplate their meaning. This is when the great symbols are born. They can take on a life of their own and constitute a kind of alternate reality, and one may become confused between what is factual and made of material reality and what is psychic or fantasy material. For a time, one may find themselves living a fictional life alongside waking life, dissociated and to an extent out of contact and withdrawn. When the libido shifts again and starts moving in a progressive direction, those symbols can be used to reorient one's life and find a new direction. Psychic energy that formerly went into one area of activity can be redirected by the symbol into a different area.

[57] Ibid., p. 170.

One often observes this reversal of psychic energy from progression to regression during transitional phases of life, such as midlife. A kind of psychological regression sets in, people lose interest in the present and return to adolescence or childhood, activating longings for things left behind or unlived in childhood. And for a time, they live a provisional life, suspended from their usual attitudes and commitments. In periods of liminality, the libido is active on the unconscious side, stirring up fantasies and visions of other possibilities. Toward the end of the transitional crisis, these symbols can be distilled into values and commitments offering new direction in the world of outer activities. One may change careers, marriage partners, or geographical locations. In the Jungian frame of understanding, such periods of regression are thought of as a normal part of development.

Jung's view of development was teleological—drawn forward, rather than driven from behind. One can consider the dynamics of the psyche from a causal, mechanistic viewpoint or from a finalistic, energic viewpoint. With regard to the latter, Jung wrote: "The flow of energy has a definite direction (goal) in that it follows the gradient of a potential in a way that cannot be reversed."[58] The psyche's

[58] C.G. Jung, "On Psychic Energy," para. 3.

libido is goal-seeking, and the goal it seeks is conscious manifestation of the unconscious. As Jung put it at the end of his life in the Prologue to his autobiographical work *Memories, Dreams, Reflections*: "Everything in the unconscious seeks outward manifestation, and the personality too desires to evolve out of its unconscious conditions and to experience itself as a whole."[59] The innate desire for wholeness, as one might describe this, determines the direction of psychic energy, sometimes in a progressive movement and sometimes through regression, but always with the same goal.

This development toward the manifestation of the psyche's wholeness is what Jung called the individuation process. The source of the energy for this is the Self, which is the author and director of the theater play that is one's life. Jung thought of the Self as the instigator of the arc of one's personal destiny.

Canalization of Libido

Jung also wrote in his essay "On Psychic Energy" of the "canalization of libido."[60] Canalization is a metaphor for the containment and direction of libido's flow. To control

[59] C.G. Jung, *Memories, Dreams, Reflections*, p. 3.
[60] C.G. Jung, "On Psychic Energy," para. 79ff.

the flow of water coming down from the mountains, for instance, people build canals. The rushing water flows to a specified destination, usually into a lake. Similarly, the flow of libido rushing from its source in the unconscious is directed by a set of structures in the conscious and semi-conscious mind and sent to a specific location where it can be used for work.

Cultures are partly responsible for the formation of these psychic canals. A culture sets rules that encourage and guide the individual toward certain types of activity and discourage other types, according to traditional patterns of behavior and attitude. As one grows up, goes to school, and develops into adulthood, one learns what is acceptable in the culture and where one's ambitions and energies can find satisfactory results. In modern cultures, there are many possible canals, but there are also some directions that are strictly forbidden or criminalized. In addition to culture, families contribute to the building up of canalization possibilities. Children of doctors often become doctors, children of lawyers may become lawyers, and so forth. Individuals have a limited amount of freedom to create new canals for themselves, although the creative element in the personality will test the boundaries and creative individuals will create new professions. Most people, however, are content to stay within the conventional canals offered when making major life decisions, such as choosing a profession or a partner.

Five Instincts

Jung also spoke about the role of instincts in the flow of psychic energy. The instincts are rooted in somatic need and impulse and are "psychized"[61] for the purposes of human expression and satisfaction. Impressed early in his career by Freud's theories and descriptions of how psychic energy is canalized into sexuality and sublimated into cultural forms, Jung later felt that Freud overstated the omnipresence of the sexual instinct and proposed instead five instincts as possible expressions of psychic energy (i.e., sublimations of basic somatic energies). He placed these on the same level, giving each an amount of potential for canalizing and directing psychic energy. He did not see one as a substitute for another.

The first is the instinct for nourishment: hunger. The body speaks its need, and the psyche responds in behavioral terms. This instinct expresses itself from the moment of birth to the end of life, though the specific forms (sucking, chewing, drinking) in which the energy

[61] C.G. Jung, "Psychological Factors Determining Human Behavior," para. 234.

is used for feeding obviously change with age and circumstance. The infant sucks milk from the breast instinctively, the adult prepares a meal and eats it, and the instinct is satisfied and becomes quiet. This is an instinct that ensures self-preservation of the individual and is certainly a primary factor in determining human behavior. Family and culture contribute to the canalization of this instinct by providing details about how to satisfy it within their various cuisines and culinary habits. Like all instincts, hunger can be distorted by neurotic conflict, with the result that the individual may suffer from an eating disorder: eating voraciously when there is no physical need, substituting food for longed-for love, depriving the body of food for the sake of social acceptance, and so forth.

The second instinct Jung cited was Freud's favorite, sexuality. Similar to the first, this instinct is subject to conditioning, in order to make it available at suitable moments in life. Also like hunger, the sexual instinct is somatically based and relies on the hormonal system that humans inherit as mammals. Its biological and evolutionary purposes are clear—to maintain and advance the survival of the species *homo sapiens*. Accompanying it, however, is a strong emotional component that serves as a bonding and attachment mechanism: love. This topic will be further discussed later in relation to the role of archetypes in the canalization of libido. In culture, the sexual instinct has many ways of expressing itself—in dress fashions, in styles of communication, in music and theater. The many varieties of sexual expression and experience have been catalogued and described by literary authors and sexologists for centuries.

When these two basic instincts are sufficiently satisfied, a surplus of energy is left for other instincts, which Jung listed as "activity," "reflection," and "creativity." These are equally rooted in the somatic base and receive their charge of energy in due course. The instinct for activity is expressed in the urge to travel or change scenery, in physical restlessness, and in the need to play. The instinct for reflection directs libido into cultural activities such as art-making, ethical conduct, and language. "Reflection is the cultural instinct *par excellence*,"[62] Jung wrote. It is dedicated to finding meaning in what one is doing and in one's life, creating a philosophy or *Weltanschauung* ("worldview"), and understanding oneself and others. Jung said the greatest passion of his life was to understand. He was hungry for Gnosis: "What is your myth – the myth in which you

[62] Ibid., para. 243.

do live?" he asked himself in perplexity at midlife. This question would call for deep reflection and lead to the creation of *The Red Book*.

Creativity is the fifth instinct on Jung's list. This instinct gets much attention throughout Jung's works and has a daimonic quality to it. It is the passion for giving birth to the new and previously unmanifest. One can see this instinct active in human history as well as in the individual. Although there is much repetition of the same patterns in personal and collective history, there is also a tremendous amount of creativity on display. Especially in modern times, we witness and experience a remarkable surge of new technologies almost daily. The human capacity for expressing creativity can sometimes be too much, becoming an out-of-control Frankenstein's monster. Jung often wrote of the torture inflicted on his life by his creative daimon. But this is the nature of creativity: it is demanding, as all instincts are.

Jung spoke about these five instincts as structures for the canalization of the flow of psychic energy. Psychic energy is sourced in the unconscious, and ego-consciousness cannot create it, only use it. The ego is dependent on the unconscious for its psychic energy like Earth is dependent on the sun for its energy. Without the sun, Earth would be dead. Just a cold rock in space.

Archetypal Images as Energy Shapers

The most influential factors for the canalization of instinctual energy are the archetypal images, which join with instinct in the psyche to direct psychic energy to its precise goal. For instance, sexual energy—experienced as a general need or longing—takes its specific direction from the potential sexual partners in one's social milieu. Such partners are "selected" through the projection of the archetypal image of animus or anima onto a specific figure, which is experienced in ego-consciousness as intense attraction to that person. When this happens, a tremendous surge of libido floods the personality, sometimes to the point of obsession (some describe this as a "magnificent obsession" created by Eros, god of love). This experience has inspired the work of numerous poets, authors and other artists, from Homer to Dante, Tolstoy, and Goethe.

The Question of Free Will

A question often debated in philosophy and psychology is how much free energy the ego has available to make decisions and choices on its own and without determination by unconscious forces and figures. Do human individuals have "free will"? If so, how much? Schopenhauer would say there is very little. The "will to be" is akin to fate, and the ego is enslaved to its service. Schopenhauer is called a pessimistic philosopher. Freud, too, is frequently labelled pessimistic, because he considered humans to be largely subject to the sexual instinct. This force of instinct can be sublimated to a degree, but when it is in favor of cultural pleasures, a strong trace of "discontent" lingers. Culture is not enough to satisfy the basic longing for sexual love, nor are other forms of love, such as friendship or community solidarity (*Gemeinschaft*). Moreover, repression of sexuality is dangerous to mental health, because it creates psychoneurosis. Acting out the Oedipal wish freely, on the other hand, is impossible in normal family life. Therefore, humans are fated to live lives of quiet (or loudly protested) frustration.

On the topic of how much freedom the ego has at its disposal to choose freely, Jung agreed with Schopenhauer and Freud that the unconscious will is the director of psychological processes and the ego's freedom is severely limited. But he disagreed that this serves only the purpose of engendering and continuing life (à la Schopenhauer and Freud). For Schopenhauer, the Will had no meaning beyond the sheer "will to be." For Freud, the meaning of the drive was limited to sexual gratification and wish fulfillment. For Jung, on the other hand, the meaning of the unconscious Will was to become conscious of itself. Jung conceived of human development as an individuation process in which the unconscious moves ineluctably toward becoming conscious. Thus, he transformed Schopenhauer's blind "will to be" into the Self's "will to consciousness," holding that the meaning of human existence in the universe is to make this possible. God needs the human mind to reach its goal of becoming consciousness. The ego may participate in this project, or it may resist and deny. If it participates, it will experience life as meaningful destiny. If it resists, it will experience life as blind fate. This is up to the ego. It has the freedom to choose—either participation or resistance. By choosing to live all five instincts consciously, the individual participates in the Divine project of cosmic consciousness.

The Transcendent Function and Ego-Self Axis

Jung felt that cooperation between ego-consciousness and the unconscious will of the Self is an essential feature of psychic health. Jung named the psychic structure created through attending to manifestations of the unconscious (e.g., dreams, visions, active imagination) the "transcendent function." This term refers to a conscious viewpoint that develops at a position of observation of both the manifestations of the unconscious and the thoughts and feelings in the realm of ego-consciousness. The transcendent function opens a way of living that consists of cooperative dialogue between the two systems: ego-consciousness and the unconscious.

Erich Neumann termed the conscious connection between ego and Self the "ego-self axis." Once established, the ego accepts the direction of the Self fundamentally and without great resistance. The word "axis" implies a strong connection of flow and agreement, such that the ego accepts its role as servant to the Self. The ego no longer seeks to dominate the psychic system but rather tries to serve the individuation process—without, however, giving up its autonomy and freedom of choice. It is not as a slave to the Self but as a willing servant that the ego relates to the superior will. To this extent, the ego has free will. It can choose to cooperate or not cooperate with the will of the Self, but it is held accountable for whichever decision it chooses. This is recognized by the great archetypal images of judgment in the afterlife.

Chapter Five

The Individuation Process

Psychology as a formal discipline apart from philosophy introduced and focused attention on the question of psychological development—that is, the development of subjectivity. Of course, it is not that psychologists suddenly discovered that humans develop and change. Since time immemorial, this phenomenon has been known and observed. The Sphinx asked Oedipus: "What creature walks on four legs in the morning, two legs at noon, and three legs in the evening?" The answer to this riddle, which Oedipus managed to answer correctly, is man (all genders included): "As a child he crawls on hands and feet, as an adult he walks on two legs, and in old age he walks with a cane." It was always obvious that a person changes physically during their lifetime. In the ancient picture, however, there was little consideration of change and development in the subjective and psychological aspects. This topic was eventually taken up by modern psychologists, who, over the last two centuries, began to study it intensively. Developmental psychology focuses on how individuals learn to cope with the exigencies of life—not primarily on the physical plane, but in their thinking, feeling, and emotional life. Development is a core feature of all schools of psychology, and for Jung it was central to his theorizing.

The notion of development at a subjective level was revolutionary. In the biblical account, for instance, the image was that humans—Adam and Eve—had been created as adults by God. When they were punished for disobedience to God's instructions and driven out of the Garden of Eden, history began. Eve bore children as infants, and human life became real as we know it today. Until the late nineteenth century, however, not much attention was given to the subjective side of a person's development. Eighteenth-century philosophers such as John Locke and Jean-Jacque Rousseau argued over the primacy of nurture or nature, but it remained for psychologists to take a closer look at the details of psychological development. Charles Darwin's concept of evolution gave impetus to psychological thinkers to apply this type of program to the development of the human psyche.

When psychological development was taken up as a topic for study and investigation by psychologists such as Stanley Hall, a new field was born. Freud, an early contributor, focused specifically on the earliest stages of psychological development in childhood. Grounded in his theory of sexuality, Freud speculated on several stages of what he called psychosexual development. The first stage was designated the "oral," with erotic excitation primarily located at the mouth of the infant as it sucks on a mother's breast. The second was the "anal," focusing on erotic stimulation at the anus. The third was the "genital," which saw erotic stimulation move to the genitals. These developments occurred in the first three or four years of a child's life. The genital stage was then followed by the fourth and final stage, the "Oedipal," when sexual excitement was directed to the opposite-sex parent, creating a situation of rivalry over the love object with the same-sex parent. The threatening figure of the same-sex adult produced anxiety, and this instilled a strict taboo in the child, giving rise to the "superego"—the threatening parent internalized. By the age of five years, the child had gone through a considerable amount of psychological development, establishing a character structure that would persist throughout their lifetime in a pattern of repetition. Freud did not consider further psychological development significant after the Oedipal stage. For this reason, early psychoanalysts considered it essential to carefully examine early childhood, so that some of these structures could be modified and the psyche could be relieved of its neurotic constrictions and allowed to expand more freely. Following Freud, Erik Erikson expanded the concept of psychosexual development to include the full lifespan across eight psychosocial stages. His theory resembles Jung's notion of psychological development as a lifetime project that is not completed in the first years, but continues throughout the course of life.

Jung called his psychological development theory "individuation," meaning "becoming what you were born to be as an individual." The theory is teleological, and in that sense Aristotelian. The basic notion is that the individual is born with a certain potential for development and proceeds to realize this potential in the project of achieving conscious wholeness. Realization of this potential depends in part on genetic inheritance—the biological codes with which one is born. But importantly and beyond this, there is a non-biological code that is rooted in spirit, rather than soma, in the realm of the archetypes. Finally, there is a synchronistic component to the individuation process. Jung was interested in astrology as a synchronistic correspondence between the positions of the stars and planets and the time and place of an individual's birth. Given these three components, he held that the eventual manifestation of the personality is a matter of unfolding potential, assisted by synchronistic moments of meaning. Freud would not have disagreed that psychosexual developments are a matter of potentials activated in time, but the other aspects of Jung's individuation theory would have been considered mystical by the creator of psychoanalysis.

For Jung, the Self is born with the infant and contains codes for psychological and spiritual development that far exceed the psychosexual. This has been called the "acorn theory of development": the acorn has the potential germ within itself to become a full grown, beautiful, massive king of the forest, given good enough conditions in the environment, and its development is a process of realizing the potential that was there from the beginning. This image was taken up and expanded upon in the brilliant work by James Hillman titled *The Soul's Code*. The tree was Jung's favorite image to symbolize the individuation process.[63] It has its roots in the earth—as the Self has in the somatic base—and it extends up into the heavens—as the Self does into the realms of the

[63] See C.G. Jung, "The Philosophical Tree," *Collected Works,* vol. 13.

spirit—thereby uniting above and below. The origins, growth, and development of the tree symbolize the individuation process in time.

Early Psychological Development

If one looks at how humans develop in their mother's womb, from the time that an ovum is fertilized by a sperm and forms a zygote (a fertilized egg that is planted in the womb of a childbearing female), one can trace how ontogeny recapitulates phylogeny. At one stage, the fetus looks like a fish with fins. Then fins become arms, the tail becomes legs, and the head grows large to allow the brain to develop. The fetus repeats all of evolutionary history in the nine months of its intra-uterine existence, thus enacting the patterns of nature inherent in the evolution of the species. This lays down the base of what Jung called the collective unconscious: a deep memory of the "two million year old man," as he referred to this foundation of the psyche.

Jung took this idea further and argued that the individual is heir to the entire history of humanity. Through the ages, what women have experienced of men, and men of women, has been recorded in the collective unconscious, forming the basis of contemporary gender relations. The human infant is born equipped with a rich heritage, which consists of features and elements common to all humans. A unique selection from all the common features, as made by parents' specific ancestral and cultural contributions—genes and memes—constitutes the individual's potential and comes to fruition in the development of that personality.

In his final book *The Child*, Erich Neumann observed that human infants are born long before they are prepared to survive on their own, and must therefore have a year of care in an "extra-uterine embryonic phase" in order "to attain the degree of maturity that characterizes the young of most other mammals at birth."[64] Human infants are hopelessly unprepared for life in this world when they are born, but they have tremendous potential if they are well nurtured through their early years. Concerning the director of development, Neumann wrote: "The total personality and its directing center, the Self, exist before the ego takes form and develops into the center of consciousness; the laws governing the development of the ego and consciousness are dependent on the unconscious and on the total personality, which is represented by the Self."[65] It is the "total personality"

[64] E. Neumann, *The Child*, p.7

[65] Ibid., p. 9.

that emerges in the individual's lifetime as a result of individuation.

Humans are born with a number of embedded codes that constitute their rich inheritance. Gary Clark, in his book *Carl Jung and the Evolutionary Sciences*, cites the revolutionary work of Marcello Barbieri, who has introduced what he calls "code biology" into the discussion of evolution. Geneticists and biologists speak of organic codes (e.g., genetic, immune, cultural), and recently they have introduced the idea of a neural code, which amounts to an archetypal code.[66] While genetic and immune codes are activated early, already in the fetus, cultural and advanced neural codes are activated gradually, later in the development process. The acquisition of language, for instance, is contained in the neural code. Barberi argues that a semiotic network develops when this code is unlocked and the child begins to understand language and other symbolic cues in their surroundings. Recognition of symbols is the result, and the potential for culture-making unfolds. Some young children show a remarkable talent for mathematics, music, and other cultural activities, as if

[66] Major, J.C., "Review Essay on Gary Clark's book, *Carl Jung and the Evolutionary Sciences*," p. 200.

by magic. The development of a psychological type, which Jung viewed as innate, also arises from one's neural code. Other archetypal patterns manifest as the lifespan continues through its stages of development, and in due course the individual's unique version of the Self emerges from the depths of the unconscious, in response to cues and opportunities in the surrounding world.

Stages of Development

Psychologists often speak of stages of development. Jung divided the lifespan into a first and a second half. In my book *Men Under Construction*, I discuss five stages of development, each dominated by a specific archetypal figure. Erik Erikson described eight stages. However, stages are not written into a code as inflexible law. Rather, stages are a hermeneutical tool for interpreting the messy multitude of phenomena in the complex process of psychological development. Stages are generalizations; individuals are unique.

Generally speaking, a stage of psychological development is marked by emotional, cognitive, and structural features that form an attitude characteristic of a particular era in a person's life—infancy, childhood, adolescence, young adulthood, mature adulthood, and old age. The stages are separated by transitional periods, such as the midlife transition (or crisis) between young adulthood and mature adulthood, and retirement between mature adulthood and old age. One might add birth and death as further transitions in the individuation process. The numbers affixed to the years in each of these stages vary according to the culture and individual. Generally speaking, the first half of life transitions into the second at about the age of forty, give or take some years. One should think of stages flexibly.

I will not go into detail here about the various stages discussed elsewhere in my writings, but rather bring the development process under the rubric of a formula: the Axiom of Maria Prophetissa. Jung was deeply impressed by the ancient wisdom held by the Gnostics and the alchemists, and was especially fond of the Axiom of Maria Prophetissa, one of the earliest alchemists who lived around the second century CE. Marie-Louise von Franz translated this Axiom as follows:

> Out of the One comes the Two,
> Out of the Two comes the Three,
> and from the Third comes the One as the Fourth.[67]

[67] M.-L. von Franz, *Number and Time*, p. 65.

The process of development begins with the One, which is named the "Pleroma" in the Gnostic text spoken to Jung by the magician Philemon in *Septem Sermones ad Mortuos* ("Seven Sermons to the Dead"). Pleroma means all that is or can be—totality, completeness, the full potential: "In the Pleroma there is nothing and everything."[68] Bringing this into the discussion of individuation, all the codes we have discussed are nascent in the Pleroma and not yet activated. The genetic and neural/archetypal codes needed for physical and psychological development exist there, which in the case of the individual represents the just-fertilized egg, prior to any differentiation of cells. It is a moment of stillness and quiet before the drama begins.

The infant begins life still somewhat in a state of psychic oneness. Erich Neumann described this as follows:

> "In the pre-ego stage, characteristic of earliest childhood, in which the ego and consciousness are still in the process of development, the polarized experience of the world with its subject-object dichotomy is not yet present. This childhood experience, which

[68] C.G. Jung, *Memories, Dreams, Reflections*, p. 279.

> is that of every individual, is the ontogenetic embodiment of the primal unitary reality in which the partial worlds of outside and inside, objective world and psyche do not exist… The child is still contained within its mother though its body is already born. In this phase there is a primary unity of mother and child."[69]

The infant does not distinguish between self and the mother's body, day and night, above and below, inside and outside, good and bad. As consciousness develops, such distinctions are made.

What follows is: "Out of the One comes the Two." This means the activation of one's developmental codes. Differentiation begins with the appearance of CREATURA, as this function is named in *Septem Sermones ad Mortuos*. This is the *principium individuationis*—the energy that creates distinctions and brings consciousness into the picture. Ego development begins in very mild form in the fetus, and once the child is born, it intensifies and continues to function over the lifetime. The Two, which result from this intervention of the individuating principle, are "opposites"—here and there, mine and yours, today and yesterday, good

[69] E. Neumann, *The Child*, p. 11.

and bad. This is the consequence of the function of ego-consciousness.

Melanie Klein, the renowned British psychoanalyst who specialized in the psychology of infants, famously wrote about how infants begin distinguishing between a “good breast” and a “bad breast”—this one has more milk and is warmer, while the other is empty, cold, and depressing. One is my friend, the other is my enemy. Later, this differentiating function makes further distinctions, such as: “I am not my brother. I am not my sister. I am not my mother. I am not my father. I am me.” The ego asserts its will forcefully over and against “the other.” Gender also becomes obvious, as children mark differences in behavior, dress, and bodies. Further aspects of identity also begin to be integrated in consciousness and take on specific forms and colors.

Within the psyche, the *principium individuationis* creates a structure of “stories” or “rooms,” with the most important being the division between ego-consciousness and the unconscious. The house with several levels that Jung dreamt of is now under construction. The conscious portion of the psyche becomes the first story of ego-consciousness and identity. There, one has a surname and a given name, an ever increasing accumulation of memories of things past, a keen awareness of things present, thoughts of things to come, gender identity, career, and relations with others. Meanwhile, in the unconscious below, the left-out or repressed portions of the psyche are active but not available to ego-consciousness. The shadow, the anima, the animus, the complexes, the unlived archetypal images and potentials, the instincts—all have a space in the house, both below and above the conscious lived-in space. The house is much larger than ego-consciousness is aware of, although sounds and disturbances bring a sense that there is more to the subjective realm than one realizes.

This stage of the Maria Prophetissa formula represents first-half-of-life development, spanning infancy to midlife. It covers the turbulence of adolescence and the achievements in young adulthood, creating defined aspirations, commitments, and judgments. Cultures recognize and enforce these habits and attitudes in their codes of conduct, and one of the main products of this stage of development is a sense of law as the ultimate arbiter. For this reason, it is sometimes called the "Father stage" of individuation. For instance, men and women may sit separately in religious ceremonies, play different roles and activities in society and family, and maintain clear gender distinctions. There may also be a sharp distinction between sacred and secular spaces, priests and laity, saints and sinners. Moses delivering the Tablets of Law inscribed with the Ten Commandments from on high is a symbol of the acme of this stage of development. However, Jesus later challenged the rules, socializing with Samaritans, eating with tax collectors, and allowing women to accompany him on his missions. In doing so, he inaugurated Maria Prophetissa's third stage of individuation.[70]

The Axiom continues with, "Out of the Two comes the Third." This announces the creation of what Jung called the "transcendent function," representing a bridge between ego-consciousness at an advanced level and the unconscious occupying other stories of the psychic house. This bonding connection (St. Augustine spoke of the third member of the Trinity, the Holy Ghost, as the love between Father and Son) leads to a new attitude representing both parts of the psyche—ego-consciousness and the unconscious. To change metaphors, the Third is the child of a symbolic conjugal union, bringing together the couple's ancestral and archetypal codes and uniting them in dedicated love for the new being (i.e., attitude) they have created.

This stage of the individuation process generally takes hold in the second half of life, although there may be premonitions earlier and delays until later. The differentiating function of the preceding phase, which divided perceptions into opposites and created separations between them, is superseded, and a larger

---

[70] For further discussion of this topic, see M. Stein, *The Bible as Dream*.

frame of consciousness opens that includes both sides held as polarities, rather than opposites. This new state of consciousness opens the possibilities for ego identity to change from the frozen state of exclusive and limiting one-sidedness to inclusive and open-ended flexibility to expand into what is not yet known. Identity is not rigidly fixed by projection and identification with others in mass-mindedness, but forms and reforms itself on acceptance of inner truth, as it emerges from the dialogue between conscious and unconscious. Goethe's famous lines in *Faust*, Part II—"Formation, transformation, The eternal mind's eternal recreation"—states the new condition well.[71] Shadow and anima/animus become family members and recognized as familiar inhabitants of the psychic household, no longer strangers and foreigners. The dynamism of new combinations of co-inhabitants produces less consistency and predictability (formation and transformation), while also bringing uniqueness and individuality in feeling and thought. Clichés drop away, and new and fresh blossoms bloom on the tree of life and its developing fullness. Typologically, superior functions remain strong, but inferior functions are recognized and brought into play alongside, which

[71] W. Goethe, *Faust*, Pt. 2, lines 6287-88.

releases blocked psychic energy, curiosity, and new types of activity. Altogether, the person presents a more rounded picture of creativity and dynamic wholeness.

The Axiom's final line, "and from the Third comes the One as the Fourth," states the completion of the psychological and spiritual development called individuation. The One that appears from the Three is a return of the original essence of the Pleroma state, now as conscious rather than unconscious oneness through projection and *participation mystique*. The latter would be a regression to what Neumann called the primal ouroboric state. Instead, this fourth stage means consciousness of the essence that was there from the beginning as the core, the individual soul. This is felt as the promise of immortality—a realization of timelessness within the three-dimensional space of temporality and development. It seals the unity that is achieved in the third stage and places it firmly in consciousness. Ego realizes its position in the home of the Self. Of this, Jung, referring to the completion of his Tower at Bollingen in old age, wrote: "it signified an extension of consciousness achieved in old age. With that the building was complete."[72]

[72] C.G. Jung, *Memories, Dreams, Reflections*, p. 225.

Transitions as Disruptors

Jung saw disruption as essential to individuation, and he had a name for the spirit of the unconscious that breaks up old patterns: "Mercurius." Without this mercurial energy from the unconscious, old patterns of identity and habitual attitudes would simply continue to run their repetitious cycles and psychic life would stagnate. The unconscious is mercurial! It has two sides: it can destroy and create, or separate and unite. This daimonic force interrupts comfortable life and sets the journey on a new course.

The individuation process has several major transitions: birth, adolescence, midlife, old age, and death. Each has features that are often experienced as traumatic or instigators of trauma. The trauma of birth is the first. Even if birth is not fraught with danger and severe suffering, it is regarded as a traumatic experience for the infant experiencing such a rude and untimely introduction to life in the world of unfamiliar objects, odors, sounds, lights, and people. The transition from intra-uterine to post-uterine life is a disruption of the warmth of enclosure in the mother's body, and the trauma is registered by the psyche and stored in unconscious memory. Infancy and childhood follow the transition of birth, with the little person now contained in the nurturing family—an extension of sorts of life in the womb. The maternal presence is dominant in this phase of life. Childhood is the era of the matriarchal, as Neumann called it.

Next, the comfort of embeddedness in the maternal during childhood is disrupted by adolescence, when the physical body undergoes major changes and the individual becomes aware of sexuality as a disruptor. This brings with it many other disruptions in the psychosocial realm. The family of origin is distanced, peer group identification takes precedence over family identity, and individual identity shifts from oneself as a "child" to something still indefinite. Liminality prevails. A complex search for identity becomes paramount, and confusion is typical. Erik Erikson's famous book *Identity, Youth, and Crisis* is focused on this period in the individuation process. It was in his adolescence that Jung had the experience of walking out of a cloud and finally feeling, "Now I am *myself*."[73] In this period of transition, strong changes in attitude disrupt family life as young people move toward independence. The later years of adolescence are often marked by dangerous, addictive, and self-harmful behaviors. Adolescents can become seemingly bipolar—manic one moment,

[73] C.G. Jung, *Memories, Dreams, Reflections*, p. 32.

horribly depressed the next. As they emerge from this initiation period, they begin to assume the identity and roles that will sustain them for the next decade or two. They become young adults.

At midlife, again, everything falls apart. Mercurius appears and instills longings and opportunities that stir the soul and lead to unexpected action. In Goethe's *Faust*, it is Mephisto who presents himself to the bored scholar and takes him out of his laboratory into a world of libidinal experience. Dissatisfaction with life as it is—with career, with family, with social identity—causes frustration and motivates change. Some people speak of a return to adolescence—driving fast cars, dancing in bars, affairs, hangovers. Others withdraw inward, become depressed, and enter therapy to find answers to their questions about the meaning of life. "Is this all there is?" they typically ask. A period of liminality ensues, which can last for several years or more. Jung documented his own midlife experience in his journals, the *Black Books*, later rendered artistic in *The Red Book: Liber Novus*. This began during his late thirties and extended throughout his forties. He told the story in *Memories, Dreams, Reflections*, in a chapter entitled "Confrontation with the Unconscious." Jung's midlife transition was a period of intense introversion and self-examination, with disruptions in family life and career. In the end, it was an initiation trial, which he emerged from as a more mature figure, producing the writing and teaching for which he is now best known. From young adulthood and his identity as a phenomenally successful psychiatrist and family man with a large villa on the shores of Lake Zurich, Jung developed into a psychoanalyst, thinker, teacher, and center of his own circle of followers in the field he named analytical psychology. Through this crisis, he forged a transcendent function that successfully brought together ego and Self in dialogue, thus forming the Three of the Axiom of Maria Profitessa. From this point onward, Jung's life and work were guided by the Three, and it remained his task in later life to extract the Four as the One—the essence of his vision—and encode it in his late writings, leaving his greatest legacy to the generations that followed.

Old age brings another time of significant disruption when Mercurius appears yet again. This is represented by *Faust*, Part II, in which Faust descends to the Mothers and engages with the archetypal figures of the collective unconscious, and finally death. This disruption is often triggered by a health crisis, as was the case for Jung, whose heart attack at the age of sixty-eight led to a visionary experience in the hospital that took him to the doors of the afterlife. This event was a major disruption in his life and inaugurated the period of his greatest work. For some people, retirement can be equally disruptive.

Major changes in daily routines and habits formed in the previous era lead suddenly and surprisingly into a period of deep and dark liminality. People suffer from not knowing what to do with their time. They may become alcoholic, commit suicide, or develop major illnesses. I was once told by an insurance company that the average life expectancy of retired CEOs is six months.

In late life, there is typically much reflection on the past, and major patterns and turning points in one's life. Individuation is driven by unconscious movements that the ego does not control. However, the course of life nonetheless appears to the reflective ego as having been guided by a unique and individual direction and purpose. When one looks in the mirror after this very long journey, so full of twists and turns, one begins to see it has created a path that can now be affirmed as destiny. This is how Jung spoke about his own life, looking back from the perspective of old age and reflecting on his story in *Memories, Dreams, Reflections*.

The challenge during this period of liminality in old age is to form a philosophy of life, a *Weltanschauung*, that draws into consciousness one's fundamental values and perspectives on the meaning of life. This gradually brings into being the Four in Maria Profitessa's Axiom, which is the One—the soul's essence, its wholeness realized in consciousness.

There are many examples of this individuation journey in both history and literature. One of the most paradigmatic is Dante's journey through the Inferno, Purgatorio, and finally Paradiso, culminating in his vision of the Holy Trinity and, beyond that, his identification with "the Love that moves the sun and the other stars" (*l'amor che move il sole e l'altre stelle*).[74] In this experience, so beautifully expressed in his magnificent poetic idiom, he becomes fully attuned with the One that has emerged out of the Three. This concluding line of his masterpiece is, as his translator John D. Sinclair wrote about the poem as a whole, "a passionate and convincing utterance of the deepest currents of his life, the pulse of his lines keeping time always with his heart."[75]

The Goal and the Director of Individuation

The ultimate goal of the individuation process is what Jung called conscious wholeness. The director of this process is the Self. The Self is the ultimate source of energy and structure: it all comes from the One. The Self is where the codes are contained—first as potential, later as activated. It is the source of the psychic energy

[74] Dante, *The Divine Comedy: Paradiso*, Canto xxxiii:145.
[75] Ibid., p. 7.

that drives the psyche along the way of individuation, toward conscious wholeness. The path involves a growing awareness, based on experience—not merely of who one is, but of *what* one is. This movement toward consciousness of the Self and psychological wholeness can be a very painful journey, as well as a very productive and satisfying one.

Jung considered the Self a God-term, in the sense that experience of the Self is equivalent to the mystical experience of the presence of and unity with God. In his writings, he often substituted one term for the other. His God was a psychological complex, not a metaphysical being, as in theology. The question Jung addressed was two-fold: "Does the human being need God, and if so, what for?" and "Does God need the human being, and if so, for what?" His answer was that individuation serves both ego-consciousness and the God complex, the Self. It expands ego-consciousness to include the Self as much as possible, and this serves the movement toward wholeness in the individual—a great value for life. Individuation also serves God by bringing consciousness to the God complex, and this serves the Self by bringing awareness into the darkness of what would otherwise remain unconscious. Humans need God, and God needs humans, and individuation brings benefits to both.

Chapter Six

The Self

Is there an invisible intelligence operating behind the scenes of the psyche? Who or what oversees the house on all its levels? Who is the architect, who the designer, who or what the manager? Is there an intelligence that keeps some semblance of order among the inhabitants and wants them to get to know each other and work together for the greater good of all? Jung divined one such agent, and named it the Self. As we shall see, the Self is a complexity—a mixture of polarities and opposites, anything but a singular, unified intelligence. Nevertheless, it does seem to be goal-oriented. Jung spoke of it as having a *telos*, a Greek word meaning "an aim, a forward-looking direction."

Jungian psychology makes a critical distinction between the ego and the Self. Although they are related and resemble one another as the center of their respective domains, the difference is immense. The ego is time-bound and limited, the Self is seemingly not. Similarly, the ego's power and authority over the contents of consciousness is significant but not final or complete, and it has no authority over the unconscious, while the Self is master of all. It is easy to confuse them because the word "self" in the English language is typically used as a reference to the ego. When we think of self-esteem, for example, we consider the ego's feeling about itself, not its feeling about the Self. The term Self is capitalized in this book (and generally in Jungian writing) because it refers to something that exceeds the ego and ego-consciousness, as God exceeds the human. It is the God figure in Jungian psychology—the archetype of archetypes, and the center and container of the whole psychic system, conscious and unconscious. When Jung spoke of the Self, he often described it is a hypothesis. By this, he meant that it is a way of rationally conceptualizing the psychological realm as a totality, in which the conscious mind is housed. The Self is the intelligence the rules over the house of the psyche.

Jung considered images of unity and totality symbols of the Self.[76] By "symbol," he meant something

[76] C.G. Jung, *Aion,* para. 59.

ineffable. A symbol is not a sign. It opens the window to the mystery, and it is the best possible representation of something that is still unconscious. Myths are narrative expressions of the symbolic world and represent it much more effectively than concepts. Therefore, it is best to look to myth for answers to the question of the nature and purpose of the Self. Myths, in particular, express an experience of the Self.

Jung also frequently referenced the mandala as another symbol of the Self. *Mandala* is the Sanskrit word for "circle," as well as a meditation device used by Hindus and Buddhists to focus the mind on the spiritual. In the history of symbolism, the circle was taken to be the perfect form. For Jung, the mandala represented the Self as the psyche's wholeness and totality.

Jung sometimes wrote of the quaternity, the number four, as a symbol of wholeness achieved. The circle represents wholeness and totality as potential, while the number four is a result of the process of differentiation and reintegration. This is the individuation process, as we have seen in earlier chapters (given classical expression in the Axiom of Maria Prophetissa). However, the number four, or the image of the square, can also represent wholeness and totality not yet arrived to the perfect level of a circle, because the opposites are still facing each other. In a square, two diagonal lines show unresolved conflict between the opposites. The corner on the upper left faces off against the corner on the lower right, and the lower left and upper right face off against each other. There are also two horizontal and two vertical lines. Thus, the square shows a tension between the opposites that have differentiated from the original One, or Pleroma. In the circle this is resolved, and there are no opposites. It is more perfect than the square. Sometimes these two images are combined. There is a square in a circle, or a circle in a square. This refers to the Self as a container of the opposites but not necessarily a resolution of the opposites—perhaps a more realistic assessment of the possibility of wholeness in life as lived in the realm of time and space.

As Jung was drawing mandalas in his spare time while on duty as Commandant de la Région Anglase des Internés de Guerre in Château d'Oex during World War I, he made an existential discovery about the nature of this invisible commander of the psyche, the Self. He wrote in *Memories, Dreams, Reflections*: "Only gradually did I discover what the mandala really is: 'Formation, Transformation, Eternal Mind's eternal recreation,' and that is the self, the wholeness of the personality, which if all goes well is harmonious, but which cannot tolerate self-deception."[77] The Self is a process of eternal formation and transformation. Does this process have a meaning? Jung would answer in the affirmative, calling it individuation.

Jung had a significant dream of the Self in 1928, representing the culmination of his midlife transformation process. The dream is commonly referred to as the "Liverpool Dream."[78] In the dream, Jung is walking through a dark street in the "dirty, sooty city" of Liverpool with several Swiss friends. They climb to a plateau where they come upon a square where several streets converge, and in the center of the square there is a round pool with an island in the center. The island is ablaze with light, and planted on it is a single tree, a magnolia. "It was as though the tree stood in the sunlight and were at the same time the source of light." Though it's dark all around, the tree is emitting light. Jung gazes at this and reflects on why a Swiss friend has chosen to move to this city: "I was carried away by the beauty of the flowering tree and the sunlit island, and thought, 'I know very well why he has settled here.'" Upon reflection on this dream,

[77] C.G. Jung, *Memories, Dreams, Reflections*, pp. 195-96.
[78] Ibid., pp. 197-98.

Jung concluded that this was the answer to the question he had been asking himself—"What is your myth – the myth in which you do live?"[79]: "I saw here the goal had been revealed. One could not go beyond the center. The center is the goal, and everything is directed toward that center. Through the dream I understood that the self is the principle and archetype of orientation and meaning. Therein lies its healing function. For me, this insight signified an approach to the center and therefore to the goal. Out of it emerged a first inkling of my personal myth."[80] Thus, the Self became the myth in which Jung lived.

The tree is a symbol of the growth of the Self in time, within the psyche of the individual. In Jung's dream, at the center of the circle the mature tree emits light, lit up by a source of energy from within. Thus, at the center there is a self-sustaining source of energy, like the sun in the center of the solar system. In a circle around the tree is the Mercurial fountain that Jung would write so fondly about years later in his essay titled "The Psychology of the Transference." It contains the water

[79] Ibid., p. 171.
[80] Ibid., pp. 198-99.

of life, and it is itself contained. This suggests unity: the Self as both center and circumference.

Jung asked himself, "Why Liverpool?" Liverpool is a large industrial city that Jung had never been to, so he understood the name to be symbolic. Just as the liver is essential for life (the word is etymologically related to the verb "to live"), the Self resides at the center of the living psyche.

Structure of the Self

Some twenty years after his Liverpool dream, Jung wrote *Aion: Researches into the Phenomenology of the Self*. This volume is about the Self as it manifests in cultural history in the form of Aeons—Platonic "months" lasting roughly two thousand years, and in the lives of iconic individuals, such as Christ. The final chapter is titled "The Structure and Dynamics of the Self," where Jung offers his understanding of the Self as an active psychological agent. For the architectural plan, he uses Gnostic mythology to create four quaternary structures stacked one atop another.

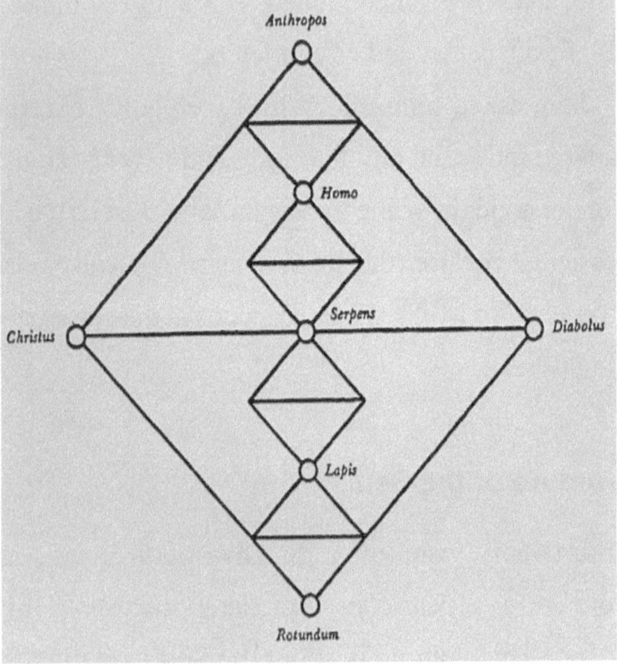

At the top sits the Anthropos Quaternio, the ideal aspect of the Self. This is made up of the best and most ideal features of the personality—one's highest and most admirable aspirations, thoughts, feelings, and behaviors. Here, the Self is at its most noble and high-minded, its most spiritual.

In this aspect, there are the figures of Moses, Moses' sister Miriam, the prophet Jethro, and Moses' wife, Zipporah (also Jethro's daughter). All four are cast as exemplary personalities.

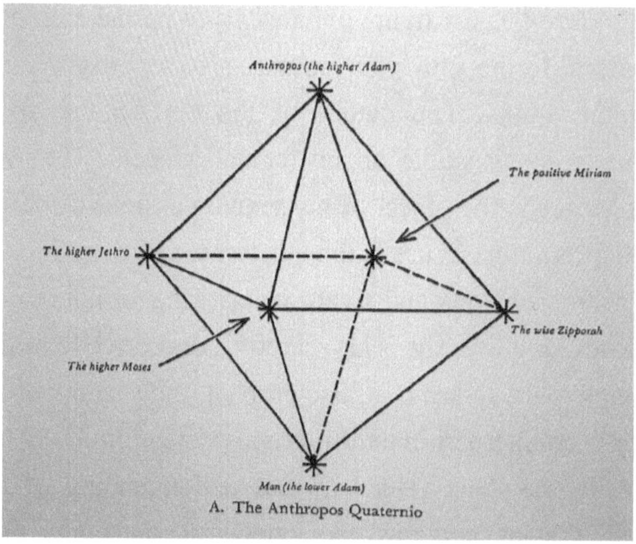

A. The Anthropos Quaternio

Below the Anthropos Quaternio is its shadow.

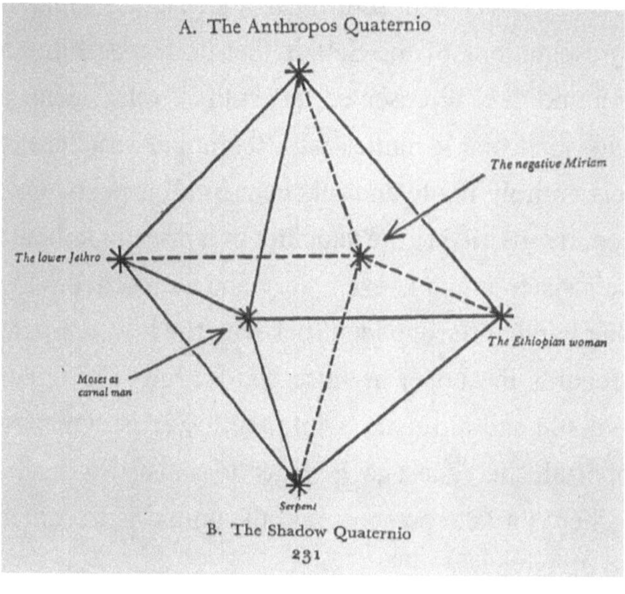

A. The Anthropos Quaternio

B. The Shadow Quaternio

231

Here lies the figure of Moses as a carnal man now married to the Ethiopian woman, also a carnal version of the anima. The figures of the Self in the upper Quaternio also take on instinctual aspects. The wife of Moses is the object of his sexual passion, while the other feminine figure in the Quaternio (Miriam, Moses' sister) is envious and rivalrous, seeking to undermine Moses' nobility. She is his secretive, deceptive feminine counterpart. Jethro is a false prophet, the shadow of his upper counterpart in the Anthropos Quaternio.

It was Jung's fundamental understanding of the Self that it contains the opposites, meaning light and dark, noble and base, masculine and feminine. What is novel and additional about these Quaternio representations of the Self is that both masculine and feminine are represented at both levels, ideal and shadow. If one identifies with the upper structure, one feels entirely noble and innocent in all aspects. One is decently married to the daughter of a priestly father, and one's sister/anima is exemplary and supportive. On the other hand, if the ego identifies with the lower structure, it regards the upper as false and untrue. The upper is idealistic and altruistic, while the lower is cynical and opportunistic. The ego is eager to satisfy its lust, the teacher is a fake persona, and the anima is treacherous and divisive.

The picture presented of the Self is that it is not a simple ideal—something beautiful, supportive, made of light and perfection, and carrying our noblest aspirations. Rather, it also contains the shadow figures in the basement of the house. People have often misunderstood Jung's concept of the Self. Part of it is ideal, but it also includes a shadow level, hosting carnality, envy, deception, and theft. The shadow enacts things that one does unconsciously, and only one's most trusted friends or bitter enemies can reveal this to them.

Below the Shadow Quaternio is the Paradise Quaternio, and this has to do with the organic and physical aspects of the Self, which are out of the range of consciousness. The Self is thus inclusive of the animal and vegetative aspects of the individual, the body and all its organs and functions. Here one enters the region of the body's foundation in the material substances of nature. This dimension of the Self introduces psychosomatic interaction, with soma and psyche in intimate relation to one another but beyond the reach of ego-consciousness. Humans are not creatures with a mind or spirit in a body, à la Descartes. Rather, they embody spirit yet live in and as a physical body. Individual humans are also very specific bodies with genetic material inherited from their recent and ancient ancestors.

Below even the Paradise Quaternio lies a further level: the Lapis Quaternio. This extends further into the material base, into the molecular and subatomic levels. Here, materia disappears into the realm of pure energy, referenced in the diagram as Rotundum. This is the increatum, the prima materia, the everlasting and eternal foundation of life itself. In modern physics, this is the quantum field. This was the critical point of Jung's collaboration with Wolfgang Pauli—Jung coming from the side of psyche and Pauli from the side of physics.

The quantum level of the psyche in the Lapis Quaternio is paradoxically connected and one with the Anthropos Quaternio. This introduces the subject of synchronicity and meaning, which I will discuss in the following chapter. At this quantum level, the solidity of matter dissolves into fluctuations and waves of energy. At the sublime heights of the spiritual dimension, all representations and images also dissolve into pure energy, as light. The light at the top and the energy at the bottom of the Self are one and the same. The organizing principle that creates substance and matter according to codes and algorithms is a function of the Self. The Self is totality and all inclusive. Smaller than small and greater than great, Jung often wrote, referencing the Bindu point of Hindu mythology—the center and the source. What this means is that humans are distinct individuals with unique features, genetic makeups, and personal histories, but they are also made of the same fundamental essence as everything that exists. This is the paradox of existence. Humans are both individual and individuated exemplars of the world of energy that underlies the stars and the planets, the plants and the rocks, the minerals, the animals, and everything that exists. Each one is a bit of the totality, of all that exists.

The individual human embodies the Self, which is at one with a much larger cosmic energy and structure, the *unus mundus*. Thus, through the Self, the individual is not only *contained* in the *unus mundus*, but they also *participate* in the *unus mundus*—the totality and wholeness at the foundation of all that exists. They are not isolated and alone. Jung described this realization as the final stage of the individuation process in the concluding chapter of his last major book, *Mysterium Coniunctionis*.

The Dynamics of the Self

What about movements of the Self? Does it move? How does it move? What is it moving toward? On this matter, Jung created a diagram showing the Self as a process.

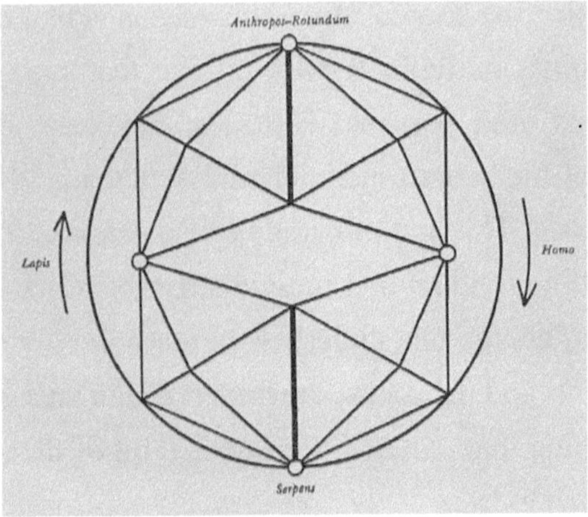

Jung began his autobiography with the sentences: "My life is the story of the self-realization of the unconscious. Everything in the unconscious seeks outward manifestation, and the personality too desires to evolve out of its unconscious conditions and to experience itself as a whole."[81] Development proceeds according to the will of the Self, not the ego, and the ego may or may not cooperate with the Self in this matter. If it does not cooperate, it experiences the will of the Self as fate; if it cooperates, it experiences the will of the Self as destiny.

As discussed in Chapter Four, the "self-realization of the unconscious" (individuation) comes about in

[81] C.G. Jung, *Memories, Dreams, Reflections*, p. 3.

stages over a lifetime. In *Aion*, Jung discussed these stages as a process of transformation within the Self—a process that takes place outside the purview of the ego, but results in conscious awareness if the ego attends to the subjective factor. To discuss this development in the Self, Jung used a formula:

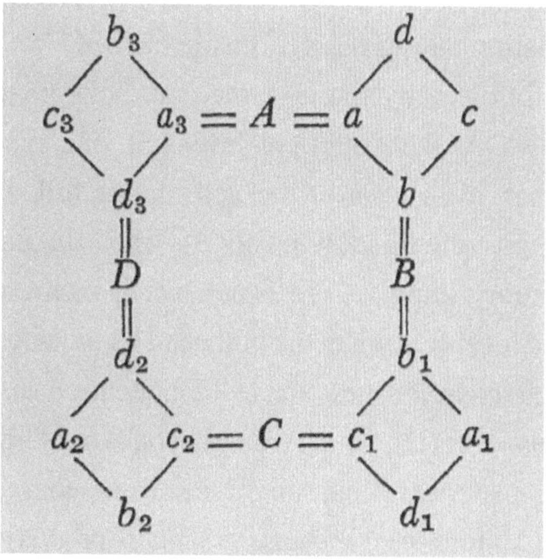

About this formula, he wrote:

> The process depicted by our formula changes the originally unconscious totality into a conscious one. The Anthropos A descends from above through his Shadow B into Physis C… and, through a kind of crystallization process D… that reduces chaos to order, rises again to the original state, which in the meantime has

> been transformed from an unconscious into a conscious one.[82]

In his further commentary, he emphasized that "the self is not just a static quantity or constant form, but is also a dynamic process… an active force. The four transformations represent a process of restoration or rejuvenation taking place… inside the self."[83]

If followed by the ego, the conscious picture runs as follows. At the Anthropos level (A), one experiences the higher, ideal level of the Self; this is followed by a descent into the Shadow level (B), when the instinctual and contrary impulses are experienced; then comes the Paradise level (C), when the body and its organic features come into consciousness and call for attention; and finally the Lapis level (D), which exists beyond one's immediate sensory experience but might occur to consciousness through intuitions, dreams, visions, or very subtle movements at the depths of one's being that are difficult to account for or specify. Jung saw a coordination of movements from one level to another that then returned to traverse the same ground, serving the ego's ever-widening consciousness of the Self as totality and wholeness.

[82] C.G. Jung, *Aion*, para. 410.
[83] Ibid., para. 411.

Some Jungian writers (particularly Erich Neumann) have used the phrase "ego-self axis" to speak of the ego's increasing awareness of the movements within the Self toward consciousness. The ego is included in the Self, of course, and ego-consciousness is a part of the Self, to a greater or lesser degree, depending on its relation to the Self. The "axis" indicates a closer and perhaps ever growing apprehension of the Self on the ego's part. How deeply can the "I" become aware of the Self? The first step is to disidentify from the contents of consciousness, the thoughts and feelings and images that inhabit this level of the psyche's house, to gain an objective view. The "I" then becomes an observer. And by opening to the unconscious and becoming familiar with the other inhabitants of the psyche's house, the "I" may develop a relation to the whole that Jung called the "transcendent function." This is the ego-Self axis. It allows the ego increasing access to the movements and developments of the Self. Such movements may be experienced in material form from the somatic or instinctual sides of life (our drives or physical requirements and pressures), or in spiritual form from the archetypal side (as ideas, visions, or symbols). Gradually, over time, the totality that is the Self becomes visible to ego-consciousness, to a greater or lesser degree. The inhabitants of the house of the psyche become familiar to one another.

In this movement toward greater consciousness of the heights and depths of the Self, the ego is required to do some serious work. To some extent, it must be passive and observant, but it must also be active in paying careful attention to the messages and tendencies that the Self is revealing, or that are being revealed within the Self, and recording them in memory. For instance, one may have a dream in which something important is revealed, but the dream is only a story or a picture—a set of images. Upon awakening and remembering and perhaps recounting the dream, one might ask oneself, "What does it mean? What is this dream showing me?" One must take the next step and interpret the dream. That is the work of the ego—to interpret the material that is made available from the Self through dreams or visions, and then to take some consequent measures in life. This is what "integration" means. It is the ego's function to integrate the material that is made manifest from the Self and make use of it in everyday existence. The Self has a strong will to realize itself in a person's life. It might communicate through a big dream, which, if properly integrated, might substantially change the course of the dreamer's life. However, if its will is continually thwarted, it will override the ego's resistance by producing unwelcome effects such as mental illness, psychosomatic illness, or synchronistic events that block or even end the person's life.

Chapter Seven

Synchronicity and Meaning

The concept of "synchronicity" entered Jung's writing rather late in his career. He developed this "principle," as he called it in the essay "Synchronicity: An Acausal Connecting Principle," slowly and meticulously over many years, in discussion with world-class scientists, including Albert Einstein and Wolfgang Pauli. The theory supporting this principle states that mind and matter have a common background and are both part of the *unus mundus* (Latin for "one world"). It has been elaborated in many books and by numerous thinkers in the years following the publication of Jung's paper in 1952, some of whom I will mention in this chapter.

A pivotal moment in the story of synchronicity occurred in 1912, when Jung met with Albert Einstein and they discussed Einstein's new theory of general relativity. The conversation did not include Einstein's mathematics, with which Jung was unfamiliar, but it confirmed Jung's intuition that common sense assumptions about the nature of reality are not correct in all contexts and do not explain or fit all phenomena, as experienced by the psyche. When Jung carefully considered the products of the unconscious, such as dreams and visions, it became clear to him that the unconscious is not limited by the usual laws of space and time. The rules of cause and effect that apply in the material world at the macroscopic level do not apply in the same way in the unconscious. Similarly, the views that Einstein and Pauli proposed about nature at the subatomic level from the side of modern physics seemed to contradict the usual notions about causality. Depth psychology and quantum physics seemed to be speaking about the same mysterious dimension of reality. Could there be a connection between them? This was the question Jung discussed with Pauli for more than a decade, before publishing his paper on synchronicity as an acausal connecting principle.

The Jung-Pauli Collaboration

From 1932 to 1958, Jung was in contact with Wolfgang Pauli, either personally or by letter.[84] At first, the

[84] See their correspondence in C.A. Meier (ed.), *Atom and Archetype*.

relationship was based on Pauli's need for psychotherapy, but it later transformed into an intensive collaboration between the two geniuses around a possible relation between depth psychology and quantum physics. The question Jung was working on with Pauli was: How do psyche and matter come together in the deep subterranean levels of quantum physics and depth psychology? Their correspondence was later published in *Atom and Archetype* (in the English translation), edited by C.A. Meier. In their letters, we can read how Jung and Pauli were engaged in formulating a vision of how depth psychology and quantum physics meet in a dimension of reality that underlies both psyche and the material world of objects. The material world studied by physics and the psychological world studied by depth psychologists are at base one world—the *unus mundus*. This realization was a revolutionary breakthrough that led to the theory of synchronicity, which Jung first presented publicly in a lecture at the Eranos Conference in 1951.

Definition and Meaning of Synchronicity

The word "synchronicity," a neologism created by Jung, is made up of two Greek roots: *syn-* and *chronos*. *Syn-* means "together," while *chronos* means "time." Thus, the word synchronicity means "together in time." Jung's concept of synchronicity refers to a coincidence in which events in mind and matter happen at the same time, either precisely or approximately. It is a coincidence between a psychic happening (e.g., a thought, dream, intuition, vision, or feeling) and a material event (e.g., an insect tapping at the window, a butterfly landing on a page, a telephone call from someone you've been thinking of, or someone knocking at your door). The two events occur simultaneously in chronological time.

What Jung added significantly to such experiences of coincidence was the factor of meaning. Importantly, synchronicity describes a *meaningful* coincidence. To add meaning to coincidence is a big step, and it is the only place in Jung's published writings that he reads as explicitly metaphysical. Generally, Jung wanted to stay away from metaphysics, because he identified himself as an empiricist. He worked with facts, not with metaphysical explanations for why facts exist. He was a modern scientist. But in speaking about the presence of meaning in temporal events, he made a much stronger claim than merely saying that humans make meaning out of coincidental events. He was arguing that meaning existed in the event, itself. It was *given*, not humanly created by the mind. It therefore had ontological status as "an act of creation in time."[85] Thus, meaning is delivered in the synchronistic event from the outside, not from the inside of the recipient's psyche. It is up to the recipient to recognize its meaning, not to make it up.

As an example of synchronicity, Jung told the story of when a beetle from his garden appeared at the window of his office while he was with a young woman patient who was just then telling him about a dream in which a piece of jewelry in the form of a scarab beetle was given to her. While Jung was listening, he heard a tapping sound on the window behind him. He went to the window, opened it, grabbed the beetle as it flew into the room, then handed it to the patient with the remark: "Here is your scarab beetle!"[86]

This surprising confluence of dream image and event in the material world changed the woman's life, he reported. She had grown up in a scientific culture with no interest in things of a religious nature, yet in her soul she was a spiritual person. This had been repressed in her by her modern education and the prevailing spirit of the times. The shock of the synchronicity released

[85] C.G. Jung, "Synchronicity: An Acausal Connecting Principle," para. 965.
[86] Ibid., para. 982.

this woman to her new life, opening her mind to the reality of the soul and the symbolic attitude.

In his paper on synchronicity, Jung included many reflections on astrology as a meaningful coincidence between planetary positions and the birth times of individuals and collectives. In a section titled "An Astrological Experiment," he studied astrological configurations among a large group of married couples for "coincident aspects" in their birth charts.[87] The results of his study were complicated mathematically, but he was quite convinced that astrological correspondences in a couple were not mere chance. They were meaningful coincidences.

Jung had a longstanding interest in astrology, as has been documented in detail by the Jungian analyst and astrologer Liz Greene. Although astrology is not an accepted science in the modern world, Jung thought it had intuitive validity based on centuries of careful observation. He also saw it as related to cultural history and wrote extensively about the Age of Pisces moving currently into the Age of Aquarius, especially in his late work, *Aion*. He did not argue for a causal relationship between the movements of planets and the life of humans,

[87] Ibid., para. 869.

but rather a meaningful coincidence (synchronicity) between them. Behind this synchronistic phenomenon, he surmised, was an archetype.[88]

The strange coincidence fascinated Jung, and he used astrology both for himself and in his psychotherapeutic practice.[89] He claimed that, sometimes, when he would get stuck and didn't understand a patient, he would ask for their birth date and draw up an astrology chart, which would help him understand them better. He found an uncanny relationship between psychic conflicts in individual patients and aspects in their astrology charts.[90]

Chronos and Kairos: Two Types of Time

Synchronicity involves time and the timing of events, inner and outer. The Greek language has two words for time: *chronos* and *kairos*. *Chronos* time is quantitative and sequential—past, present, future, moving along like a stream. However, there are certain moments in chronological time that are qualitative and very special,

---

[88] Ibid., para. 900.

[89] See L. Greene, *Jung's Studies in Astrology* and *The Astrological World of Jung's Liber Novus*.

[90] C.G. Jung, "Synchronicity: An Acausal Connecting Principle," paras. 897-899.

in that they represent the transcendent present in time. For instance, in the Bible, Paul uses the phrase, "in the fullness of time" (πλήρωμα του χρόνου)[91] to speak of the birth of Christ. This is *kairos*. *Kairos* moments are symbolic. They are moments when something takes place that has significance and meaning beyond the mere marking of a moment in temporal time, as when we state the hour or date of an event: "He was born on December 25, 3 BCE." There is a vertical dimension as well as a horizontal, when the eternal breaks into the temporal: "He was born in the fullness of time."

Kairos moments are mythological, and they are unpredictable. They transcend our understanding of cause and effect. Humans cannot comprehend the cause, only the effect. *Kairos* moments are also synchronistic. A virgin gets pregnant and gives birth to a child at a moment in history when the Platonic Ages are moving into a new Aeon, and the child born will come to symbolize the Age of Pisces. When Jung spoke about synchronicity, he was speaking about *Kairos*—moments in time with special significance and meaning, whether on the small scale of the individual or the large scale of

[91] Galatians 4:4.

the world. Often, these moments mark turning points of personal or historical significance.

Parapsychology

A related area of research that fascinated Jung was parapsychology and paranormal phenomena. In his paper on synchronicity, he referenced J.B. Rhine's experiments on extra-sensory perception (ESP) at Duke University in the 1930s and 1940s as offering support for such phenomena. In Jung's view, synchronicity played a role in ESP. Rhine's evidence of correct guesses of symbols on Zener cards by people in separate rooms exceeded statistical probability, to the extent that the experiments were considered strong indication that telepathy should be respected and studied further. However, Jung would add synchronicity as a factor: the guesses were meaningful coincidences and not necessarily transmissions of information via unknown channels. He took the same view of this as he did of the astrological relations between planets and humans: they're synchronistic.

Mysterium Coniunctionis and the Union of Opposites

Synchronicity describes the union of opposites, when psyche and matter come together at a specific moment in time to deliver a message of meaning. When Jung presented his paper on synchronicity at the Eranos conference in 1951, he spoke about his last great work, *Mysterium Coniunctionis* (Latin words meaning "mysterious union" or "conjunction"). He had been working on this book for ten years, and it would not be published for another five. In it, he described the goal of the individuation process as the creation of a unified psyche no longer sharply divided between ego-consciousness and worlds inner (the unconscious) and outer (the material world), but rather one with a steady flow of information passing between them without defensive obstruction. In the moment of synchronicity, the opposites brought together are psyche and matter. This contributes to the unification of psyche and world in an experience of *unus mundus*, representing the third and final stage of Dorn's development plan, as discussed in chapter four. In *Mysterium Coniunctionis*, the opposites of mind and matter are represented by classical pairs, such as King and Queen, and Sun and Moon. Their unification represents the union of mind and matter.

Individual and General Synchronicity

In the discussions between Jung and Pauli, they spoke about two types of synchronicity: individual and general. Jung was primarily interested in individual synchronicity, referring to the synchronistic experiences of individuals that deliver meaning to their life and become part of their individuation process.

In general synchronicity, synchronistic events occur outside of human subjectivity, in the evolution of the natural world. Such events may involve human beings indirectly, but not subjectively. Pauli felt that synchronicity had been playing a role in evolution even before humans existed. In evolutionary theory, there are moments when changes take place in genetic codes that look like accidents but turn out to be highly significant for the next stage of evolution. To Pauli, these were synchronistic events in the general sense.

Theological Parallels and the Sense of Destiny

What's behind synchronicity and the meanings it delivers? In mythology, it would be the gods. In Christian theology, it is God. Jung grew up in a Christian family and knew the biblical stories of creation and divine intervention very well. But he put all of that aside when he did his scientific work.

Nonetheless, the notion of synchronicity seems very close to the theological ideas of grace, divine will, and God's interventions throughout history.

In Jung's discussion of synchronicity, there are no theological explanations as such. However, there is a similarity in the notion that the world, both subjective and objective, is organized according to a plan that underlies human psychic life and the material world. When one follows the thread of synchronicities in one's life, there appears to have been a plan in place—an underlying program. One may have thought one was making decisions consciously and by free will, but in fact one was following a program that one can only now see emerging through synchronistic moments—chance meetings and encounters with people of significance, life-changing books placed in one's hands, messages received by chance, dreams, and so forth. When Jung wrote about this, he called it destiny. Others might call it fate. Is there a "hand" above one's head that leads and guides the paths one pursues? Jung would call this the Self, the archetype of archetypes.

Conclusion: Synchronicity, the Capstone of Individuation Theory

Jung often expressed the intuition that his life followed a destined path—that he was meant to do what he did and to leave the legacy he did. By following his own path through dreams, visions, active imaginations, and synchronistic experiences, he produced a body of work that is significant for humankind. Jung's theory of synchronicity is the capstone to his work on the individuation process. Individuation is the realization of the Self in an individual's lifetime, and that realization comes about through both a natural unfolding of the innate potentials that are written in code at birth and through synchronicities (*kairos* moments), which give life specific meaning and direction. People become what they were meant to be, and psyche and matter cooperate in forging their destiny.

Chapter Eight

Jungian Psychoanalysis – A Brief Account

In the previous chapters, I have discussed the theory of analytical psychology as created and elaborated by C.G. Jung over the course of his long career first as a psychiatrist, then as a Freudian psychoanalyst, and finally as himself, a Jungian psychoanalyst in practice. His theories grew without exception from his experiences, relating to his work as a doctor of souls. He was above all a physician, as is clear throughout his writings. His official persona was his professional title as doctor, but he had a burning passion to understand the psyche in all its aspects. I have called him a map-maker because of his explorations of the vast territory of the psyche, both conscious and—especially—unconscious. From these explorations, which were deeply experiential, he developed his theories, and he used his theories as guidelines for the treatment of his patients.

In this concluding chapter, I want to discuss applications of the theories of analytical psychology in the practice of Jungian psychoanalysis, as these were developed by Jung and later expanded and elaborated by his successors.[92] When students are trained as Jungian psychoanalysts in the institutes that have been set up around the world for this purpose, they are instructed in how to use these theories practically. Here, I will speak briefly about their use with respect to diagnosis, treatment, and prognosis.

Diagnosis and Assessment

In making a diagnosis or assessment of a potential patient for analysis, the first question the Jungian psychoanalyst asks is about the level and quality of the person's ego functioning.[93] As the center of consciousness, the ego has the essential role of managing consciousness in such a way that a strong degree of stability and balance is maintained. Ideally, the subject will take in information about the world

[92] For a more complete discussion of this topic, see M. Stein (ed.), *Jungian Psychoanalysis* and M. Stein, *The Practice of Jungian Psychoanalysis*.

[93] See Chapter One for a discussion of ego-consciousness.

around—the social and natural worlds—as well as from the inner world of complexes, and make use of this information without becoming overly perplexed or overwhelmed by this information. However, this is not always the case. What one faces in clinical practice are issues of ego inadequacy and failure, when the subject cannot cope with the perceptions and the emotions they generate. Instead, the ego falls back on defenses such as dissociation, projection, denial, and repression, or collapses altogether in panic and psychosis. In this case, the ego is not functioning well enough in its role as moderator, reality-tester, and manager of psychic material flooding into consciousness. The Jungian psychoanalyst seeks to assesses the capacity of ego-functioning in the present life of the patient as a first step, before making a more complete diagnosis.

A related consideration in the assessment has to do with persona development.[94] Is the persona of the patient adequate to their situation and station in life at the present time? Depending on the age of the person and their stage of life, one expects that a certain level of persona development has been achieved. Otherwise, an insufficiency may be creating problems such as

[94] See Chapter Five for a discussion of persona.

avoidance of social situations, interpersonal difficulties at school or work, or challenges in intimate and familial relations.

Persona development is in turn related to the deeper issue of identity. In some patients, there may be a question of gender identity. This is an issue that is very current today, especially among adolescents and young adults. A sense of identity has to do with a feeling of "me-ness." Is the patient confused about who or what they are? What does the next step in their life look like? This is an issue that comes up especially during transitional phases. Adolescence, midlife, and old age are periods when one's sense of identity changes significantly, and for a time, confusion is common.

Another feature in the assessment process relates to typology. Typical problems here are underdevelopment of the superior function, false development of a superior function due to conditioning and cultural pressures, and extreme one-sided development of typological features. Typology shifts and changes during a lifetime, as individuation proceeds. In the assessment phase, the analyst considers which of the functions have been developed and which have not, and which attitude is perhaps too dominant or undeveloped.

Then one goes a bit further in the assessment and considers the effects on consciousness of the unconscious and the complexes. Some Jungian analysts use diagnostic tests like the word association experiment (WAE) or the Thematic Apperception Test (TAT) to investigate intrapsychic factors in disturbances to ego-consciousness. In the early sessions of an analysis, the question of what the major complex is that causes the most difficulties for the patient takes a prominent position in the analyst's thinking. One might conclude that it is, for instance, an abandonment complex—fear of being abandoned due to traumatic experiences in the person's early life.

The assessment also includes something about the patient's major libido investments at the present time. The analyst will listen for where major amounts of psychic energy are being spent. Some areas may be considered relatively healthy if not over-loaded, while others, such as obsessions and compulsions, are considered more psychopathological. A lot of energy can be used up in, for instance, an eating compulsion. One thinks about food issues throughout the day, considering constantly when to eat, how much to eat, whether to snack or not to snack, and so forth. Addictions (tobacco, cocaine, exercise, etc.) are also heavy libido investments that absorb a huge amount of available psychic energy. These habits override the ego's will and decision-making capacities and control the flow of libido as they will.

The assessment also considers major projections. Where does this person project shadow? Where does the anima or the animus land? At this stage of the therapeutic process, these items are only noted. Later, they will become a major feature of analysis and discussion, as effort is made to become more conscious about the psyche in all its features. The question asked in the assessment phase is: How conscious is the patient of shadow and anima or animus projections and their sources?

Perhaps the most important feature in a Jungian diagnosis and assessment concerns where the patient is in the individuation process. As I have written in the first chapter of *Four Pillars of Jungian Psychoanalysis*, this is a constant question in the back of the analyst's mind throughout the analytic process. At the start of analysis, the analyst will wonder if the stage of individuation the patient has reached matches their chronological age. According to the schema for individuation as worked out by Jung and his successors, the normal lifespan is divided into several stages, each of which has its distinctive challenges and requirements.[95] The

[95] See Chapter Four for details.

assessment will consider whether and to what extent the patient's psychological development has kept up with their chronological age or gotten blocked somewhere. Some people remain in childhood when they should be in adulthood, or they become developmentally stuck in adolescence when they are already well into the second half of life. The answer to this question will become a central guide for the type of treatment that is considered optimal for advancing the patient's individuation.

Finally, Jungian analysts often look at the initial dream as diagnostic. A patient brings a dream that they've had either shortly before beginning the analysis or shortly after it's begun. This dream will contain a message about the major issues that lie ahead in the analysis. In retrospect, if one looks back at initial dreams after working with a patient for six months or a year, one can see that the dream anticipated issues and themes that then became salient in the sessions that followed. The initial dream is taken to be part of the diagnostic phase of treatment, while also indicating something about what the treatment can or should be.

Treatment

A patient's treatment is based very much upon the psychological assessment made by the analyst in the first sessions. Every person who comes in for psychotherapy is unique. The Jungian analyst has this very much in mind when they meet with a patient for the first time. They do not assume too quickly that they know about the patient's subjective life, and they try to empty their mind of assumptions and avoid quick diagnostic snapshots that might turn out to be limiting. And yet, the treatment must be based on a feeling for the patient's major issues, problems, weaknesses, and strengths. Not every patient is able to withstand the impact of analysis, so the analyst is cautious about entering too deeply into psychological territories that the patient is not ready to explore.

Jung told the story of a case in *Memories, Dreams, Reflections* of a man who presented himself as very normal. He was a medical doctor who came to him for analysis and wanted to train with him to become an analyst. The man was living a very normal life. As Jung described, he had a normal household and normal income, normal children, everything was normal. But before Jung went far into analytic explorations of the patient's unconscious, he asked for some dreams. Based on a dream that the man brought, he concluded that it would be dangerous for this man to go too deeply into this territory of the unconscious, because of what was lurking there: "I knew all I needed to know – here was a latent psychosis! I must say I sweated as I tried to lead him out of that dream. I had to represent it to him as something quite innocuous, and gloss over all the perilous details."[96] If this man were to delve too deeply into his unconscious, there was the possibility that his ego would be shattered by the experience of the confrontation. Based on his experience as a psychiatrist, Jung chose to talk the patient out of further analysis and out of training to become an analyst. He was well situated in a comfortable ("normal") situation, where his ego defenses were adequate, and he should just continue living his life at that level of individuation.

The Analytic Relationship

The German word for "treatment" is *Behandlung*. Literally, this means "hands on to handle something." If you were to go into treatment with Jung, you would be "handled." Jung was a very active analyst. He was not a "sit back, wait, and let anything happen" type of analyst. He took hold of the situation because he felt responsible for his patients and their well-being. If he saw that they were in danger psychologically, he did

[96] C.G. Jung, *Memories, Dreams, Reflections*, p. 135.

everything he could to anticipate the negative event and prepare the patient to deal with it.

Jung recommended that the analyst get involved in and become part of the process. This can be dangerous for the analyst, because the analyst also has complexes and psychic weak spots. The analyst must know their own strengths and weaknesses before engaging deeply in handling a patient who might have the capacity to trigger their core complexes or infect them with psychic illness. Jung wrote about the infectious nature of psychological conflict. It's as if the patient has a cold, and the therapist catches it. Infections are not only somatic, but also psychic. Jung was aware of the danger that analysts encounter when they engage in depth with patients. Stepping into the treatment room poses a risk for both analyst and patient, because the unconscious of both may be powerfully constellated in the relationship.

When the analyst enters the treatment with commitment, they step into the waters of the unconscious, alongside the patient. Jung wrote about this graphically in his work, "The Psychology of the Transference," using the alchemical pictures from the *Rosarium Philosophorum* to illustrate the analytic process. The *Rosarium* tells the story of alchemical transformation through the images of a King and a Queen who meet fully clothed, then remove their clothes and enter a bath together, where they become sexually intimate and produce a child who represents the product of the process, the Self. Jung used these pictures and texts to discuss analysis as a process that travels through death of the old personas and identities to birth of a new life in the Self. He regarded this as a mutual transformation in both analyst and patient.

From his writings and the reports of his patients, it is clear that Jung became deeply engaged with his patients. His ego-consciousness and complexes were deeply involved. The analytical relationship is multi-layered and complex, as Jung showed in his essay on the transference. On the one hand, there is the conscious-to-conscious relationship, whereby the analyst's ego-consciousness relates to the patient's ego-consciousness in the manner of having a verbal dialogue. This level is conversational, and the arrangement of persons is face-to-face. Both are engaged in the conversation, and the rules of practice regarding boundaries, contracts, and ethics are respected. On the other hand, there is also unconscious-to-unconscious engagement, whereby the unconscious becomes activated in the analyst, and it becomes activated in the patient as the treatment proceeds. The complexes and archetypal energies in both become engaged through mutual projection.

Working with Dreams

Working with dreams is an essential feature of Jungian psychoanalysis. Here, I use the phrase "working with" rather than "interpretation," because the method is dialogic and not top-down. Dreams are an important source of information about the unconscious background of the patient's past and present, and about the relationship between analyst and patient. Jung described cases in which he even revealed his own dreams of patients to patients. Most Jungian psychoanalysts are hesitant to do anything similar, for several reasons. First, the patient must be of a suitable level of development, and second, the relationship must be firmly established and strong before the patient can receive the analyst's dream material usefully. Jung used his dreams to help patients get out of the impasses or abysses into which they had fallen. The examples that he gave showed that this had the effect of freeing his patients to individuate further. An analyst's dreams about a patient are not necessarily indicative of the analyst's depth of engagement in their treatment, but they can signal that the analyst is missing something about the patient. This is how Jung understood his dreams about patients—namely as compensations to his waking attitudes about them, telling him he was not seeing them correctly. When he brought these dreams into sessions, it was as though he were telling his patients, "I've not seen you before, and this dream corrects my vision of you. I now see you more accurately."[97] Doing so could create a new relationship of deeper respect and feeling between Jung and his patients, because confessing his mistakes and showing his dreams indicated to them his commitment to their growth and progress.

Active Imagination

The second important method that is used in Jungian treatment is active imagination. Again, this is not for everyone—particularly not for people whose ego strength is not able to engage with strong energies in the unconscious. Active imagination is a conscious and direct engagement with the unconscious. While the dream is a spontaneous happening over which the ego has no control or responsibility, active imagination is undertaken voluntarily and under the control, at least initially, of the ego. The ego decides to engage in the activity with unconscious content, or simply open itself to the unconscious and see what steps forward, and subsequently engage with it. Active imagination is used

[97] See C.G. Jung, *Memories, Dreams, Reflections*, p. 139.

as a part of psychotherapeutic treatment to openly bring ego-consciousness into contact with the unconscious. It is generally considered by Jungian psychoanalysts to be essential for furthering a patient's psychological and spiritual development. It brings about a greater sense of oneness, unity, and wholeness in the personality, as one's ego and unconscious forge a closer, more conscious, connection. Sometimes this contact works a seeming miracle of healing. Jung reported that, for some patients, their "apparent morbidity drops away the moment the gulf between the ego and the unconscious is closed."[98]

Over time, and with consistent practice, active imagination builds up a picture of one's inner world and inner life that is a companion to waking life. This is not a replacement or substitute for everyday life, nor is it a defense against suffering. It does not provide an escape, but rather companionship.

Work in analysis with dreams and active imagination attempts to advance the individuation process in the sense of making the Self and its internal developments more conscious. The Self wants to become conscious and incarnate, and attending to dreams and practicing

[98] Ibid., p. 144.

active imagination are methods of facilitating this. During treatment, a patient may become aware of inhabitants in several levels of the psyche's house. For instance, they may discover the shadow within and not only in projection. In dreams, they may find figures that represent or symbolize their own shadow impulses and tendencies, which are normally projected onto people in the world around. The point is that the shadow is usually experienced as something *out there*, but over the course of treatment, it becomes experienced also as something *in here*.

Having a strong enough ego capacity to suffer the shadow is important. This is why ego strength is such an important requisite for deep analysis. The stronger the ego, the more pain and suffering it can bear, and the more pain and suffering it bears, the stronger it also becomes. We grow through suffering the consciousness of our own shadows.

There are also the anima and the animus. To discover these within relieves a person, to some extent, of projecting them onto the people around them. Knowledge of their features and qualities as parts of the Self relieves a person of the compulsive need to be with an anima or animus figure in order to feel more alive and whole. If they are experienced as an inner resource, they do not need to be as present in the world around.

And one will have better relationships with other people because they are not the recipients of projected archetypal figures, but rather real people. Archetypal projections create expectations that are unrealistic and doomed to collapse.

The Role of Synchronicity

Synchronicity plays a role in both diagnosis and treatment. One observes synchronistic events as one moves through the process of an analytic treatment. Normally, people have experiences in which co-incidences are noted but not given much attention or value. They are only curiosities. In analysis, however, one looks at them carefully, interrogating them for meaning. In Jung's theory, the most important thing about synchronicity is that it delivers meaning that was not created consciously. Through reflection, one discovers the meaning of the synchronicity, and this can be life-changing. One can look upon meeting a particular analyst as a synchronistic event, for example. Why did it happen that such important work and intimacy came about with this specific person? Also, from the analyst's side, meeting with certain patients is synchronistic. There is a saying among Jungian analysts that one gets the patients one needs for further development and individuation. These are meaningful encounters in life with persons who can have a significant impact. Analysts also pay attention to synchronicities that happen within sessions. Sometimes a patient is telling a dream and there is a coincidental event in the surroundings that carries meaning, as in Jung's story of the scarab beetle at his window.

Prognosis

Prognosis is the concluding step in the analytic *opus*. When analysis comes to an end, the analyst is left with a question: Can this person develop further? What is the prospect for future individuation in this person's life? Based on what has been experienced during analysis, the analyst will be equipped to make a prognosis on the individuation potential of the patient.

"This person has reached their limit" would be one type of prognosis. In other cases, the analyst might see much potential. In still other cases, it may be a sad prognosis. A prognosis grows out of the experience of analysis with the patient and how it has developed over the course of the time it has run. It is an educated guess based on the experience of the analyst.

Conclusion

This is a very brief and compact description of how Jung's theory is put to work in a practical way in psychoanalysis. Theory grows out of analysis and practical work, and it also assists in the work. The capabilities of the analyst are continuously under development.

References

Abramovitch, H. (2016). "The Search for a New Ethic: Professional and Clinical Dilemmas." In E. Shalit and M. Stein (eds.), *Turbulent Times, Creative Minds. Erich Neumann and C.G. Jung Caveat in Relationship*. Asheville, NC: Chiron Publications.

_____. (2023). "Henry Abramovitch in Dialogue with Murray Stein, 'The Shadow and the Search for a New Ethic.'" In M. Stein (ed.), *The Shadow and the Problem of Evil. Five Examinations*. Asheville, NC: Chiron Publications.

Bair, D. (2003). *Jung. A Biography*. Boston, MA; New York; London: Little, Brown and Company.

Barbieri, M. (2015). *Code Biology. A New Life Science*. Springer.

_____. (2024). *Codes and Evolution: The Origin of Absolute Novelties*. Springer.

Beebe, J. and Falzeder, E. (eds.). (2014). *The Question of Psychological Types. The Correspondence of C.G. Jung and Hans Schmid-Guisan, 1915–1916.*

Translated by E. Falzeder. Princeton, NJ: Princeton University Press.

Beebe, J. (2016). *Energies and Patterns in Psychological Type*. New York, London: Routledge.

Carus, C.G. (1846/1970). *Psyche*. New York: Spring Publications.

Clark, G. (2025). *Carl Jung and the Evolutionary Sciences. A New Vision for Analytical Psychology*. London: Routledge.

Csikszentmihalyi, C. (1990). *Flow. The Psychology of Optimal Experience*. New York: Harper & Row.

Dante, A. (1939/1961). *The Divine Comedy: Paradiso*. Translated by J.D. Sinclair. New York: Oxford University Press.

De Angelo, X. (1952). "Comments on a Doctoral Thesis." In W. McGuire and R.F.C. Hull (eds.), *C.G. Jung Speaking*. Princeton, NJ: Princeton University Press.

Ellenberger, H.F. (1970). *The Discovery of the Unconscious: The History and Evolution of Dynamic Psychiatry*. New York: Basic Books.

Erikson, E.H. (1968). *Identity Youth and Crisis*. New York: W.W. Norton & Company.

Freud, S. (1930/1961). *Civilization and its Discontents*. New York: W.W. Norton & Co.

Goethe, J. W. (2001). *Faust.* Translated by Walter Arndt. New York: W.W. Norton & Co.

Grattan-Guinness, I. (1982). *Psychical Research: A Guide to its History, Principles and Practices: In Celebration of 100 Years of the Society for Psychical Research.* Aquarian Press.

Greene, L. (2018). *Jung's Studies in Astrology*. London, New York: Routledge.

Hillman, J. (1997). *The Soul's Code*. New York: Bantam.

Jung, C.G. (1953–1983). *Collected Works*. Edited by Sir H. Read, M. Fordham, G. Adler, and W. McGuire. 20 vols. Princeton, NJ: Princeton University Press.

_____. (1897/1983). "Some Thoughts on Psychology." *The Zofingia Lectures. Collected Works,* Supplementary vol. A.

_____. (1902/1957). "On the Psychology and Pathology of So-Called Occult Phenomena." *Collected Works*, vol. 1.

_____. (1909/1975). "New Aspects of Criminal Psychology." *Collected Works*, vol. 2.

_____. (1916/1991). *Psychology of the Unconscious: A Study of the Transformations and Symbolisms of the Libido. Collected Works*, Supplementary vol. B.

_____. (1921/1971). *Psychological Types. Collected Works*, vol. 6.

_____. (1928/1969). "On Psychic Energy." *Collected Works*, vol. 8.

_____. (1929/1961). "Freud and Jung: Contrasts." *Collected Works*, vol. 4.

_____. (1934/1954/1968). "Archetypes of the Collective Unconscious." *Collected Works*, vol. 9i.

______. (1936/1964). "Wotan." *Collected Works*, vol. 10.

_____. (1936/1969). "Psychological Factors Determining Human Behavior." *Collected Works*, vol. 8.

_____. (1943/2015). Bernardini, R., Quaglino, G.P., and Romano, A. (eds.). *The Solar Myth and Opicinus de Canistris. Notes of the Seminar given at Eranos in 1943*. Einsiedeln: Daimon Verlag.

_____. (1946/1966). "The Psychology of the Transference." *Collected Works*, vol. 16.

_____. (1952/1954/1969). "Answer to Job." *Collected Works*, vol. 11.

_____. (1954/1969). "Synchronicity: An Acausal Connecting Principle." *Collected Works*, vol. 8.

_____. (1953/1966). *Two Essays on Analytical Psychology. Collected Works*, vol. 7.

_____. (1954/1967). "The Philosophical Tree." *Collected Works*, vol. 13

_____. (1956/1970). *Symbols of Transformation. Collected Works*, vol. 5.

_____. (1959/1968). *Aion: Researches Into The Phenomenology of the Self. Collected Works,* vol. 9.

_____. (1961). *Memories, Dreams, Reflections.* Recorded and edited by A. Jaffé (ed.). Translated by R. Winston and C. Winston. New York: Vintage Books.

_____. (1988). *Nietzsche's Zarathustra. Notes of the Seminar Given in 1934–1939.* 2 vols. Princeton, NJ: Princeton University Press.

_____. (1977). *Mysterium Coniunctionis. Collected Works,* vol 14.

_____. (1997). Douglas, C. (ed.) *Visions. Notes of the Seminar Given in 1930–1934 by C. G. Jung.* 2 vols. Princeton, NJ: Princeton University Press.

_____. (2009). *The Red Book: Liber Novus. A Reader's Edition.* New York and London: W.W. Norton & Company.

Jung, C.G. and Riklin, R. (1904/1975). "The Associations of Normal Subjects." *Collected Works*, vol. 2.

Major, J.C. (2025). "Review Essay on Gary Clark's book, *Carl Jung and the Evolutionary Sciences: A New Vision for Analytical Psychology.*" *International Journal of Jungian Studies*, 17:2, 195–214.

Maram, E. (2016). *Psychopathy Within.* Asheville, NC: Chiron Publications.

Mason, T. (2010). *Forensic Psychiatry. Influences of Evil*. Totowa, NJ: Humana Press.

Meier, C.A. (ed.) (2001). *Atom and Archetype: The Pauli/Jung Letters 1932–1958*. Princeton, NJ: Princeton University Press.

Neumann, E. (1973). *The Child: Structure and Dynamics of the Nascent Personality*. London, New York: Karnac.

Otto, R. (1916/1958). *The Idea of the Holy*. Oxford: Oxford University Press.

Plato (1948). "Symposium." In Buchanan, S. (ed.), *The Portable Plato*. New York: Viking Press.

Schopenhauer, A. (2010). *The World as Will and Representation*, vol. 1. Cambridge: Cambridge University Press.

Schweizer, A. (ed.). (2023). *C.G. Jung Letters to Hedy Wyss 1936–1956*. Einsiedeln: Daimon Verlag.

Shamdasani, S. (2003). *Jung and the Making of Modern Psychology: The Dream of a Science*. Cambridge: Cambridge University Press.

Singer, T. and Kimbles, S.L. (2004). *The Cultural Complex: Contemporary Jungian Perspectives on Psyche and Society*. Hove, New York: Brunner-Routledge.

Stein, L. and Stein, M. (2025). “The Role of the Brain in Individuation.” *Journal of Analytical Psychology,* 2025, 70, 3.

Stein, M. (2020–2025). *Collected Writings.* Edited by S. Buser and L. Cruz. Asheville, NC: Chiron Publications.

_____. (1983/2020). *In MidLife. Collected Writings*, vol. 2.

_____. (ed.). (1995). *Jung on Evil.* London, New York: Routledge.

_____. (2010). *Jungian Psychoanalysis.* Chicago, IL: Open Court.

_____. (2016). “Erich Neumann and C.G. Jung on ‘*The Problem of Evil.*’” In E. Shalit and M. Stein (eds.), *Turbulent Times, Creative Minds. Erich Neumann and C.G. Jung in Relationship.* Asheville, NC: Chiron Publications.

_____. (2018/2022). *The Bible as Dream. Collected Writings*, vol. 6.

_____. (2020/2021). *Men Under Construction: Psychological Transformations in the Life of Men. Collected Writings*, vol. 3.

_____. (2022). *The Practice of Jungian Psychoanalysis. Collected Writings*, vol. 4.

_____. (2022). *Four Pillars of Jungian Psychoanalysis. Collected Writings*, vol. 4.

_____. (ed.). (2022). *Jung's Red Book for Our Time: Searching for Soul in the 21st Century. An Eranos Symposium*. Asheville, NC: Chiron Publications.

_____. (2023). "The Shadow and the Problem of Evil." *Collected Writings*, vol. 7.

Stein, M. and Arzt, T. (eds.). (2017–2020). *Jung's Red Book for Our Time: Searching for Soul Under Post-Modern Conditions*. 4 volumes. Asheville, NC: Chiron Publications.

Virgil. (2020). *The Aeneid*. Translated by Shadi Bartsch. New York: Random House.

Von Franz, M.-L. (1974). *Number and Time*. Evanston, IL: Northwestern University Press.

Zumstein-Preiswerk, S. (1975). *C.G. Jung's Medium: Die Geschichte der Helly Preiswerk*. Munich: Kindler Verlag.

www.ingramcontent.com/pod-product-compliance
Lightning Source LLC
LaVergne TN
LVHW090402210926
848480LV00002B/421
* 9 7 8 1 6 8 5 0 3 6 9 3 5 *